Stepping Up

a journey through the

Psalms of Ascent

Beth Moore

LifeWay

Nashville, Tennessee

Published by LifeWay Press®
© 2007 Beth Moore

ISBN 9781415857434
Item 005091397

This book is the text for course CG-1303 in the subject area BIBLE STUDIES in the Christian Growth Study Plan.

Dewey decimal: 223.2
Subject heading: WORSHIP \ BIBLE. O.T. PSALMS—STUDY

To order additional copies of this resource: write LifeWay Church Resources Customer Service; One LifeWay Plaza; Nashville, TN 37234-0113; FAX order to (615) 251-5933; call toll free (800) 458-2772; e-mail *orderentry@lifeway.com;* order online *www.lifeway.com;* or visit the LifeWay Christian Store serving you.

Printed in the United States of America

Leadership and Adult Publishing
LifeWay Church Resources
One LifeWay Plaza
Nashville, TN 37234-0175

Contents

To my beloved "Raleigh Girls" —

The concept for this Bible study dropped from Heaven right into my heart as God prepared me to speak to many of you at a Living Proof Live event. I had one of the greatest times of my entire ministry life with you that weekend. God used your vocal enthusiasm for our emphasis on the Psalms of Ascent to turn a two-day conference into a full-scale Bible study. Thank you for being so excited that I literally could not help doing something more with the subject matter. I have no higher esteem to give anyone than this: I loved Jesus more when I left you than when I came. Stay in His Word, Sweet Raleigh Girls!

Love always,
Beth

About the Author

Beth Moore has written best-selling Bible studies on David, Moses, Paul, Isaiah, Daniel, John, and Jesus. Her books *Breaking Free, Praying God's Word,* and *When Godly People Do Ungodly Things* have all focused on the battle Satan is waging against Christians. *Believing God, Loving Well,* and *Living Beyond Yourself* have focused on how Christians can live triumphantly in today's world. Beth has a passion for Christ, a passion for Bible study, and a passion to see Christians living the lives Christ intended.

In *Stepping Up* Beth invites you to join her in aspiring to reach a new level of relationship and intimacy with God. May you be blessed by your journey.

Introduction

This is my first in-depth study on the psalms. Until now I haven't had a clue how to approach a book of 150 chapters in a time frame that wasn't too daunting. When God introduced me to this compilation of 15 psalms (120–134) and began to show me its place as a "psalter within a psalter," I couldn't wait to throw myself into it. The psalms have been constants throughout my entire adult life. I've turned to them many times when I've had feelings that needed biblical expression. Sometimes I needed to word overwhelming gratitude and praise. Other times my sorrow, fear, or anger needed expression. The psalms have invited me to safely pour out my heart to God. Eugene Peterson describes the psalms so well:

> "There is no literature in all the world that is more true to life and more honest than Psalms, for here we have warts-and-all religion. Every skeptical thought, every disappointing venture, every pain, every despair that we can face is lived through and integrated into a personal, saving relationship with God—a relationship that also has in it acts of praise, blessing, peace, security, trust and love.
>
> "Good poetry survives not when it is pretty or beautiful or nice but when it is true: accurate and honest. The psalms are great poetry and have lasted not because they appeal to our fantasies and our wishes but because they are confirmed in the intensities of honest and hazardous living."[1]

I expect nothing less than a new level of intimacy with God through these pages. I ask you to settle for nothing less as well. The more we bare our souls to God, the safer we'll feel *with* Him and the closer we'll draw *to* Him. If we'll let Him, God will turn each of us into true worshipers, fully released to celebrate Him, reverence Him, laugh with Him, cry with Him, and even make our complaints to Him. God is our hiding place. Our shelter through the storm. Let's find Him in a way we've not yet known.

Our study will cover six weeks, each with five days of homework. No matter who you are or where you've been, this study is for you. You don't need any religious training or previous Bible study to participate in this journey. At the same time, the psalms will challenge the serious student of God's Word to take the next step with God.

Although I welcome you to join us for the video sessions whether or not you participate in the homework, I tell you without hesitation that the most important part of your experience will happen in the time you spend alone with God through these pages. That's where you'll hear His voice in the most personal way. We have 30 days of homework ahead of us, allowing us to spend two days on each psalm. (The only exception is the first Psalm of Ascent because we will need to spend our initial day introducing the psalms in general.) Although other assignments will differ from psalm to psalm, we will practice three consistent approaches on each day of homework that introduces a new psalm. Soon you'll know them by heart, but until then I've placed these instructions in the introduction so you can easily reference them. Read them now and then refer to them as directed in the study.

Our Three Approaches to the Psalms of Ascent

Each time we introduce a new psalm we'll practice three approaches. We'll …

Say it, Work it, & Pray it.

The exercise I'm about to suggest is critical to reaping the greatest harvest from our study, so I urge you to participate if at all possible. This is how: When the psalm is introduced …

First, we'll *say it.* I'll ask you to read the psalm first in the Holman Christian Standard Bible as our choice for a solid study text. I will then ask you to read the psalm in one other version. It may either be another major translation, The Amplified Bible, or one of the modern paraphrases such as The Message to add a more current texture and help you form word pictures. If at all possible, read the psalm in both versions aloud. You'll process it much better than with silent reading alone. You will also become more aware of the rhythm and flow of the song.

Second, we'll *work it.* Go to work on the specified psalm in ways I'm about to suggest and add to them your own creative methods. Make your own notes around it. You can mark the page in your workbook in ways you might never have room or desire to do in your Bible. On each day a psalm is introduced, please complete the following:

- Circle every reference to God or title given to God. If you really want to get creative, use one color of ink for all words or titles that refer to Him and another for all other notations. In the formal versions (as opposed to most modern paraphrases), when you see references to *Lord,* the Hebrew transliteration is a form of *Adonai,* emphasizing God's lordship and His position as Master. When you see references to *LORD* (all caps), the Hebrew *YHWH* emphasizes His position as covenant maker and keeper. When you see references to *God,* the Hebrew

Elohim emphasizes His position as universal Creator. Keeping these emphases in mind will make the name considered in its context all the richer.

- Underline any word or phrase that stands out to you, speaks to you, or even confuses you. Put a question mark beside anything you don't understand.
- Convey in the margin any time the psalmist's words or descriptions remind you of a comparable experience in your own life. I have written phrases like "When Mom died" or "when captive" to the side of various verses that reminded me of how I felt or how God met me during those times. When something reminded me of my children, I've written their names beside the verse. When I read something in Scripture I deeply want for my husband, I'll sometimes write "Keith!" Other times when I've wanted to write in a code that no one else but God and I could decipher, I've written dates or years when something happened in my life comparable to the psalmist's description. Get the idea? Jot phrases any time you can relate to something quoted in one of the psalms.
- Compare the writing styles of the two translations. When you've particularly enjoyed a parallel, draw arrows from the phrase in the HCSB to the corresponding phrase in the additional translation.
- Share with your small group your own ideas to enhance the reading.
- Do whatever increases your learning experience and comprehension level!

Overachievers can get on a Bible resource Web site (such as *http://bible.lifeway.com* or *www.blueletterbible.org*) and bring up the King James Version with Strong's numbers, discover the original transliteration of the Hebrew, and learn what the word means. Be creative! Be studious!

Third, we'll *pray it*. As we progress through the two lessons on each psalm, we'll personalize various portions, enabling you to conclude the second lesson by writing a rendition of your own based on the concepts we learned. You'll find blank lines at the end of the coinciding lesson for this purpose. If a psalm doesn't apply to you in your life right now, perhaps it reflects something you experienced in the past. If so, write your own psalm as a past-tense memorial as David often did.

When we've concluded our attentions to a particular psalm, you'll be directed to turn to the back of your workbook, locate the graphic of the 15 stairs, and write in a phrase or brief sentence on the corresponding stair what you'll most take with you from that psalm.

Thanks so much for coming along, Dear One! It wouldn't be the same without you! Thoroughly enjoy your God as He seeks to take you to the next step.

Christ is life!
Beth

viewer guide

Introductory Session

Welcome to a study of the Psalms of Ascent. Hopefully you will find this study of the Word of God completely unique from others we may have shared. Today we'll stand together at the starting line of the path God has paved for us and catch the vision for what's ahead. This entire session is dedicated to answering two questions: What are the Psalms of Ascent, and what do they have to do with us?

1. The Psalms of Ascent are a compilation of _____*15*_____ psalms extending from Psalm ____*120*____ to ____*134*____ .

2. The Hebrew transliteration for *ascent* is *ma'aloth* meaning __*to*__ __*go*__ __*up*__.

3. Through the centuries the Psalms of Ascent have shared the following three associations:

• Read Deuteronomy 16:16-17. These songs were sung on the pilgrimage to the Three _____ _____ (compare Ex. 23:14). Because of these commands the Three Great Feasts were also called the _____ Feasts. Cross-reference Psalm 84:5-7 and Hebrews 12:18-19,22-24.

• According to the Talmud[1], the 15 psalms somehow developed a connection to 15 steps of the temple. (See the temple diagram.) So strong is the association with steps of some kind that the Septuagint, Latin Vulgate, and Jerome labeled each psalm "a _____ of the _____." Consider the following proposal of a daily practice as we seek to "go up" to the next level with God: Those of us who desire to participate will take our _____ on our _____.

• These songs were sung by _____ returning to Jerusalem after Babylonian _____.

1. The collection of ancient Rabbinic writings relegating much of orthodox Judaism. Reference to 15 steps: b. Sukk. 51b; b Mid. 2:5.

Week One
Where Will My Help Come From?

Principal Questions

1. What five tones or words would you choose to describe the psalmist's state as he approached God?

2. What does Psalm 142:1-2 give you permission to do?

3. What connection do you see between taking an uncertain journey and wanting a reminder that your covenant LORD is the uncontested Maker of heaven and earth?

4. How does Psalm 91:4 depict the closeness of God's shelter?

5. What parallels from Ephesians 2:11-22 apply to lessons you learned about the peace of Jerusalem?

ADMISSI
With this ticket

Day One : Worship on the Way
Day Two: Woe to me
Day Three: The Lord Your Keeper
Day Four: The Lord Is Your Shelter
Day Five: The Peace of Jerusalem

Day One
Worship on the Way

I am ecstatic that you decided to come along with me on this pilgrimage through the 15 Psalms of Ascent. As we pour over Psalms 120–134, God has a private agenda for each of us. However, I believe He has the following goals for all of us:

- God desires to dramatically change our outlook on daily life.
- God wants to raise us to a higher plain of worship and service.
- God wills to usher us to the next step in our personal journeys with Him even if we have to press through the thickest forest to get to it.

I hope you can participate in our video sessions and have already viewed our introduction. But in case you haven't, allow me to set the stage. Even if you participated, you will still glean from a brief review.

One of the commitments we're making is to take a moment every day to get down on our faces before God. Yes, I mean all the way down on the floor with our backs to the sky, as my husband often says.

The prospect poses a legitimate problem for some of you. I have the joy of hearing from women taking part in the Bible studies who are into their 80s and who might be afraid that if they got down, they'd never get up. I can respect that! Others may be younger but have serious back or knee injuries that make the exercise painful or virtually impossible. Needless to say, those with physical limitations are gladly exempt; however, if this applies to you, consider a modification that expresses the same idea. Perhaps you could sit at a table and put your face down on it for a moment or at a couch and go facedown on the armrest. The idea is to demonstrate reverence and surrender, however you personalize it.

God will undoubtedly honor your expression. Though getting down on our faces first thing in the morning has the tremendous advantage of setting the tone for the day, I don't want to teeter on legalism by imposing that kind of requirement. The point is to practice a facedown posture of reverence and surrender at some point every day of our six-week journey and preferably around the time you're doing your homework. Here's the reason: In God's economy, the way up is down.

What does 1 Peter 5:6 say to you?

_____

_____

TODAY'S TREASURE

"In my distress I cried unto the LORD, and he heard me."
Psalm 120:1, KJV

If one of our priority goals is to press to a higher place with God, we could do few things that would enhance our progress more than bowing low so God can lift us up. Humbling ourselves before God is not the same thing as self-hatred. Humility is the natural posture of anyone who grasps the greatness of God. While you're on your face before God each day, put your own words to your personal act of reverence and surrender. Try something as simple as the words I prayed this morning while face-down on my back porch:

Lord, I thank You again this morning that You are still God upon the throne of all creation. You are holy. Mighty beyond comprehension. So worthy of my praise and the outpouring of my life's energies. Today I gladly give myself to You. I am convinced that You are always for me. Obedience to You will always mean Your very best for me. I'm so grateful that I can come boldly and without shame before Your throne because I pray all these things in Jesus' name.

The whole practice probably took no longer than a minute. Sometimes I linger longer if I'm particularly distressed or filled with a heightened cause for praise. Sometimes I abbreviate if I forgot to leave my dogs in the house and they're fretting over my head, fearing I'm dead. This morning, however, was a regular kind of day that I could live to honor an extraordinary kind of God.

After that moment facedown on the concrete, I got up and had a seat at the table and continued my regular prayer and devotional time. See what I mean? Going face-down every day is neither hard nor time consuming, yet I will do very few things in the course of a day with greater spiritual significance. I am convinced that the difference in this present journey through the Psalms of Ascent will be like night and day. Bottom line? We want to go up. So we need to go down.

This morning I remembered something humorous that happened to me a few weeks ago. When the time came to get ready for work and put on my makeup, I positioned myself in front of the bathroom mirror to start what Keith calls the beautification process. Suddenly I took a double take. A cluster of tiny grains loosed from the concrete floor of my porch were stuck to my forehead. I couldn't help but laugh out loud. With my dismal history, life works best for me with forehead to the floor and floor to the forehead. Perhaps you've made similar discoveries about your own life. If so, you and I will have rich company on this journey together, and if we see a little gravel on each other's foreheads, we'll just praise God for settling a very important issue with us: We're desperate for God.

This study is about going from here to there. About making real progress. Simply put, if you want to get on with it, whatever "it" may be, you can rest assured you're signed up for the right journey. Has it been a while since you've had a good jolt to jump-start your journey again? Do you feel a little stuck in this area or that? Truth be told, are you a little bored? Unmoved? Or is your deepest heart's desire to move on with God but the obstacle before you is titanic? Do you want to learn to take the high road in that ongoing situation or conflict that so often tempts you to take the low road? All of these are great reasons to take part in this series, but really, any will do.

Perhaps you just wanted to study God's Word and weren't seeking any particular theme or subject matter. Sometimes we don't know why we're on a certain road with God until miles have made their way to the soles of our feet.

What brings you to this study? _____

_____

If we could only see beyond the veil of the natural world, look upon our true surroundings, see the kingdom in the distance, and behold the face of Jesus Christ, we'd realize the tragedy of ever settling into a stagnant, mediocre relationship with God. You and I have places to go. People to meet. Dragons to slay. Foes to defeat. If God had already taken us everywhere He intended, we'd be at His glorious feet by now. That you and I are still here drawing terrestrial breaths tells us that God still has appointments for us. As we contemplate our immediate future with Him, let's reflect a bit on our pasts.

About how long has your journey with God been thus far? _____

How did it begin? _____

_____

PERSONAL QUESTION

Based on all you've experienced with God …
What excites you most about your next adventure with Him? _____

_____

_____

What scares you most about your next adventure with Him? _____

_____

_____

Our study has the wonderful potential to heighten our anticipation and diminish our dread. These psalms were meant for regular pilgrims just like us. Along our focused study of the Psalms of Ascent, we'll learn a number of things about the psalms in general and get to know the book itself a little better.

"The Greek word *psalmoi* means 'songs,' from which comes the idea, 'songs of praises' or 'praise songs.' "[1] Like much of what we sing in our places of worship, the psalms are poetry put to music. The tunes were not recorded, but you can be virtually sure we'll hear the original scores in heaven. Though often all attributed to David, the shepherd-king, God inspired a handful of other authors to add substance and circumstance to the volumes penned by the man after God's own heart.

Glance at the end of the Book of Psalms. How many psalms are there? _____

Of this number, please note the following designations of authors:

- 73 bear the name of David.
- 12 are attributed to Asaph, a Levite musician David appointed to lead worship with singers under Asaph's tutelage.
- 10 are attributed to the sons of Korah who were also temple singers. The psalms designated by the names of Asaph or the sons of Korah could also refer to a hymnbook from which they commonly sang.
- 2 are believed to have been written by Solomon.
- 1 was written by Moses.
- 1 was written by another singer named Heman.
- 1 was written by an additional singer named Ethan.
- The remainder are anonymous. Many of the undesignated songs probably fell from the pen of David, the sweetest psalter of Israel. The entire book of 150 psalms is associated with him for good reason. Surely he more than any other person in Scripture is used of God to teach us how to materialize our worship.[2]

Go back and circle each of those numbers and underline each of the names to enhance them in your memory.

Along the way the psalms were divided into five "books" believed to correspond to the five books of Moses (Genesis–Deuteronomy).

Book One: Psalms 1–41
Book Two: Psalms 42–72
Book Three: Psalms 73–89
Book Four: Psalms 90–106
Book Five: Psalms 107–150[3]

How did the traditional groupings come about? See one primary way for yourself. Look up the following Scriptures that fall at the conclusions of each "book" and write enough of the wording in the space provided to help you remember them:

Psalm 41:13 _____

Psalm 72:19-20 (Be sure to note both verses.) _____

Psalm 89:52 _____

Psalm 106:48 _____

Psalm 150:6 _____

What do they have in common? _____

No matter how you described it, you probably just noted the practice of a wonderful thing called a "benediction," a concluding blessing of grand finale praise drawing a time of focused worship to a close. Each of these verses places an exclamation point on its coinciding book of songs. The psalms are ample in number and almost endless in application. Though he considered himself bereft of description, I have found no words more expressive of the psalms' gift of wide reach than John Calvin's in his commentary introduction. Read and relish!

"The varied and resplendent riches which are contained in this treasury it is not easy matter to express in words; so much so, that I well know that whatever I shall be able to say will be far from approaching the excellence of the subject. … I have been accustomed to call this book, I think not inappropriately, 'An Anatomy of all the Parts of the Soul'; for there is not an emotion of which any one can be conscious that is not here represented as in a mirror. Or rather, the Holy Spirit has here drawn to the life all the griefs, sorrows, fears, doubts, hopes, cares, perplexities, in short, all the distracting emotions with which the minds of men are wont to be agitated."[4]

What if those very emotions became avenues of worship rather than distraction? How do you think something like that could be possible? Give an example.

_____

_____

Underline what John Calvin called the Book of Psalms in the quote above.

Let's conclude by seeing for ourselves how quickly we can affirm in Scripture what John Calvin described. Flip through the psalms, allowing your eyes to quickly scan the pages and to fall on expressive words.

PRINCIPAL QUESTION

What five tones or words would you choose to describe the psalmist's state as he approached God? Write the reference beside it. I'll get you started:

Distress, Psalm 4:1 _____   _____

_____   _____

_____

The psalms as a whole have much to teach us, not the least of which is that honesty is not inconsistent with worship. Go back once more to Calvin's excerpt. Circle any descriptions that sound like you right now. You and I are going to learn to worship God with our whole hearts—whatever their present conditions—as we pick up our weary, blistered feet and take the next step with God.

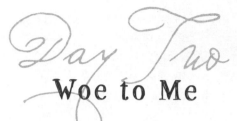

Woe to Me

I'm so glad you're back! Have you had a chance to get down on your face before God today? If you haven't, the day isn't over. If you're in a private place, perhaps now is a great time. Remember, it just takes a moment, but its repercussions last an eternity. If you're at work, you might wait until you get home. After all, picture the scene. What if one of your coworkers called 911? And what if the one person who wasn't staring a hole through you tripped over you and broke his nose? You know what the Word of God says about not causing someone to stumble. Imagine if you made a person stumble face-first into the copy machine and his hateful expression was captured in print. That's not how we want to make God famous in our workplace.

I guess these kinds of things are on my mind because the maintenance people in our building constantly come into my office to work on my faulty air-conditioning vents. They don't knock, and trust me when I say that a person enters this office at his or her own risk. Demonstrative person that I am, if I'm distracted or hurt about something when I need to be writing, you could easily walk in the room and find me facedown, telling God goodness knows what that's none of your business. If I've had a breakthrough or God has shown me something wonderful, I might instead be up on my feet in the middle of a praise leap. I could get a complex just thinking about what property management says about me. The point is that we demonstrative types not only have the capacity to make people at work stumble but we also may cause them to break a limb. Just be careful out there. Praise can be dangerous.

The instructions I'm going to share with you now are vital to our journey. They will explain the study methods you will apply to each psalm as it is introduced. Please turn now to the introduction and look for the portion called *The Three Approaches*. Read them very carefully and refer to them again and again in the days to come until you recall them easily as a psalm is introduced.

Did you get the three approaches? Write them in this space:

_____ ⟶ _____ ⟶ _____

Now let's give them a try. The 15 chapters that comprise the Psalms of Ascent begin purposefully with Psalm 120. For the remainder of our lesson we will consider its content and timely concepts. Ask Christ to open your understanding and sharpen your ability to apply what He shows you; then *say it, work it,* and at the conclusion of today's lesson, *pray it.*

TODAY'S TREASURE

"Woe to me that I dwell in Meshech, that I live among the tents of Kedar!"
Psalm 120:5, NIV

PSALM 120 (HCSB)

A Cry for Truth and Peace
A song of ascents.

1 In my distress I called to the LORD,
   and He answered me:
2 "LORD, deliver me from lying lips
   and a deceitful tongue."
3 What will He give you,
   and what will He do to you,
   you deceitful tongue?
4 A warrior's sharp arrows,
   with burning charcoal!
5 What misery that I have stayed in Meshech,
   that I have lived among the tents of Kedar!
6 I have lived too long
   with those who hate peace.
7 I am for peace; but when I speak,
   they are for war.

PSALM 120 (The Message)

A Pilgrim Song

1-2 I'm in trouble. I cry to GOD,
   desperate for an answer:
   "Deliver me from the liars, GOD!
   They smile so sweetly but lie through
   their teeth."

3-4 Do you know what's next, can you see
   what's coming,
   all you barefaced liars?
   Pointed arrows and burning coals
   will be your reward.

5-7 I'm doomed to live in Meshech,
   cursed with a home in Kedar,
   My whole life lived camping
   among quarreling neighbors.
   I'm all for peace, but the minute
   I tell them so, they go to war!

By now hopefully you've (1) *said* Psalm 120 and (2) *worked* Psalm 120 according to our earlier instructions. Now let's talk it through. At first glance Psalm 120 may seem like a peculiar launching pad for a pilgrimage taking us to the next level. Actually, our starting block could not be more perfectly suited to jump-start our journey.

The Psalms of Ascent begin with a distress call. Not a bad place to start a journey. Sometimes the best motivation we'll ever have for going someplace new is distress over someplace old. Life may come easier to some people than others, but even in the best of times it's hard. Life can also change in the blink of an eye. The morning started fine; then you got to work and learned your job was deleted. Or you got to the doctor's office and it was more serious than originally thought. Or you thought you and your spouse were fine and found out through a third party you weren't.

"In my distress I called to the LORD, and He answered me." Could you characterize your present season as distressing in any way? If so, have you called to the Lord and told Him all about it? He certainly already knows, but God's first priority is relationship, not just emergency response. He's looking for close interaction with you. As you write your own psalm, call out to Him deliberately and passionately, Beloved.

Glance ahead to Psalm 120:5 and compare it to *Today's Treasure*. The first phrase in the New International Version is priceless.

Glance back to the beginning of this lesson; then fill in the blank accordingly:

"_____ to me that I dwell in Meshech, that I live among the tents of Kedar!"

The psalmist began his pilgrimage by giving way to a classic "woe is me" moment. Before he could make future progress, he tried to take present stock. It wasn't pretty.

Though the two place names are foreign to us, what Meshech and Kedar represent certainly is not. The psalmist meant that he was a long way from home and from where he wished to be—that he felt like an alien. Can you relate? On the other hand, the application may not be figurative for you. You may live in a literal city or town that is very challenging for you.

I never want you to write anything down that could get you in trouble or devastate someone if he or she read it. However, the psalms call us to very personal areas of expression and worship. To reconcile the need for both discretion and expression, as you work through the personal application exercises throughout all six weeks, answer each question, but when necessary, use vague or what I like to call "code" language.

With that in mind, do you feel like an alien in some part of your living or working environment? O yes O no *If so, why?*

_____

_____

If you're like me, you may have to deal with authentically difficult people on a fairly regular basis. But in defense, do you tend to return difficult for difficult? Explain.

_____

_____

We may have relationships with some people who don't highly prioritize integrity and who fight dirty, but somewhere along the way we've got to quit getting in the mud with them. Part of making our ascent is learning to take the high road. The process can begin by voicing to God the pain you've suffered on the low road.

Today those of us who need it are going to accept biblical permission to have a "woe to me" moment with God concerning some difficult environments we're enduring. Sometimes we just need to get some things off our chests and know someone has listened. We're going to address with God some virtually impossible circumstances and personalities that surround us as we're trying to keep our spiritual act together.

Some of you feel as if you have so much stacked against you in your daily environment that it's no wonder you've lost your joy—your holy passion, your effectiveness. For instance, my godly friend's husband was an unbeliever. He never beat her or was unfaithful to her, but too frequently he was as mean as a snake. One Sunday morning she asked him if he'd move his truck so she could pull out her car and go to church. He refused. He finally moved it but not in time for church. He moved it in time for her to head to a counselor's office and figure out what she could do.

My friend was a prime candidate for bringing a "woe to me" to her faithful God who not only hears her complaint but also hears her heart. I've also heard testimonies of women who are mean-spirited to their husbands. You'd be astonished to know how many husbands have written me along the way about their wives. If they were telling the truth, their wives probably needed a good scolding. We also know that moms can be mean-spirited to their children just like dads. Some Christian bosses, both men and women, are insufferably arrogant. Difficulty has no gender bias.

PRINCIPAL QUESTION

What does Psalm 142:1-2 give you permission to do? _____

_____

Bringing our complaint before God is much more effective than dumping it on other people. We often end up spewing poisonous blame, condemnation, and bitterness on people yet rarely get what we think we need from them. Don't misunderstand me to say that we shouldn't take prayerful opportunities to speak the truth in love and address things that concern us in our living environments. Of course we should. I'm simply saying that we don't always have to be as calm and careful when we pour out our complaints to God. We can say things like this:

Woe is me that I dwell in _____ and live among the tents of _____.
I don't want you to fill in those blanks with your pen; I want you to fill them in silently before your trustworthy God. Simply share with Him what—if anything—makes your living or working conditions difficult. When you articulate this concept in your concluding psalm, write in vague or "code" terms if necessary.

I'm sick of being deceived, Lord. Save me from liars (author's paraphrase). Note how much ink the relatively brief first Psalm of Ascent gives to the psalmist's complaint about liars. You'd have to live under a rock not to be hurt sometime by another person's dishonesty. Deception truly is the native language of this natural world.

Try to look beneath the deceptive actions into the potential need. What do you think are the roots of deception in an untruthful person?

_____

_____

Let's ask ourselves if we have some of those same root issues and if we've let God treat them. As I look back on my childhood, my adolescence, and my young adulthood, I must sadly face areas in which I harbored and practiced deceit. I hid my deep wounds and insecurities with lies. I'm not that person anymore, but I'll wisely not forget her.

I've also been hurt badly by the deceit of others. You too? If so, how?

Take some time to pray. Voice to God the distress deception has caused you.

Loren Crowe writes, "The metaphor of the tongue as a destructive organ that launches words as one launches arrows, or whose effects are like those of burning coals."[5] Consider the final pleas of the psalmist in Psalm 120. *Lord, I'm weary of living or working continually around people who thrive on conflict. I want peace, but they love a battle* (author's paraphrase). Is this you? As I consider my past, it's certainly been me! Spend a moment telling God where constant conflict is getting to you. Exhausting you. In just a moment as you write your rendition of this psalm, be as forthright as you can without using specific names.

Some people just love a good fight. Customarily, I'm not one of them. However, if someone keeps trying to pick one, I'll finally—and sometimes gladly—give it. You see, we can start out loving peace among those who hate it and before we know it, we can become just as contentious as they are. At the end of the day every environment is a learning environment. Just like boxers in a ring, we learn how to fight.

As you and I seek a higher road to walk on planet Earth, the time may have come to unlearn some things and to sign up for some new lessons. Avoiding conflict is not the solution, but learning how to deal with it is. If we're willing, God will teach us. He will use His Word, He will use His Spirit, and on a good day He will use His people.

Meshech and Kedar were good places to begin our journey upward. We must be honest about where we are before we can journey effectively to where we want to be. Thanks for coming along. Conclude by writing your own rendition of Psalm 120 and writing a phrase or brief sentence on the corresponding step on your stair graphic.

My Psalm 120

Day Three
The Lord Your Keeper

Our text for the next two days is Psalm 121. I'm not sure a more beautiful song of such brevity appears on the pages of holy writ. Give added attention to this eight-verse chapter because it will be our memory verses for this series. I'm setting a goal of two verses per week. This will cause us to have the psalm memorized by the midpoint of the fifth week, leaving us a week-and-a-half to solidify it in our memories and our final two sessions to say it together. For that reason I ask that we memorize out of the Holman Christian Standard Bible so we can say it in unison then.

Don't get stressed if memory work doesn't come easily to you. No one will be put on the spot to say it by herself or feel left out if she doesn't participate. At the same time, don't be afraid to try. Grab some index cards and write one verse on each card. Start with two cards this week and take them with you everywhere you go. Picture what the words describe so they'll take shape in your mind's eye. Next week add two more. Even if you don't get every word in order, God will profoundly bless your focused meditation, causing the truths to take up residence in you. OK, it's time for you to *say it* and *work it*. At the conclusion of day 4, you'll *pray it*. Review the instructions under *The Three Approaches* in the introduction then proceed accordingly.

TODAY'S TREASURE

"The LORD protects you; the LORD is a shelter right by your side."
Psalm 121:5, HCSB

PSALM 121:1-8 (HCSB)

1 I raise my eyes toward the mountains.
  Where will my help come from?
2 My help comes from the LORD,
  the Maker of heaven and earth.
3 He will not allow your foot to slip;
  your Protector will not slumber.
4 Indeed, the Protector of Israel
  does not slumber or sleep.
5 The LORD protects you;
  the LORD is a shelter right by your side.
6 The sun will not strike you by day,
  or the moon by night.
7 The LORD will protect you from all harm;
  He will protect your life.
8 The LORD will protect your coming and going
  both now and forever.

PSALM 121:1-8 (Hans-Joachim Kraus)

1 I lift my eyes up to the hills. From where does help
  come to me?
2 Help comes to me from Yahweh, who has made
  heaven and earth.
3 He does not let your foot waver, your keeper
  does not sleep!
4 Behold, neither sleeps nor slumbers the keeper of
  Israel!
5 Yahweh is your keeper, Yahweh is your shade above
  your right hand!
6 By day the sun does not strike, nor the moon by
  night.
7 Yahweh protects you against all harm, he protects
  your life.
8 Yahweh protects your going out and coming in from
  now on and forever.

Every time I memorize and solicit the Lord's help throughout the process, He causes the portion to come to me. If I don't pray, it's like pulling teeth. Hopefully our study will also cause Psalm 121 to mean something special to us, making memorization much easier. Now to the passage.

First of all, notice the shift from first person references in verses 1 and 2 to the exclusive use of second person pronouns throughout the remainder of the psalm. Mark this transition on the psalm. Such a feature is not unusual in the psalms, and in this particular case it has influenced many scholars to view Psalm 121 as a liturgy. From this perspective the traveler or "pilgrim" speaks in the first two verses and a worship leader or priest responds in the remaining verses.

Pour over all eight verses and note each reference that suggests the psalm was written on or about a literal journey:

_____

_____

Some scholars suggest that the first two Psalms of Ascent beautifully depict the pilgrimage of the dispersed Jews back to Jerusalem, either at the conclusion of captivity or at the time of year for the pilgrim feasts. Follow their thought process: Psalm 120 unfolds with the pilgrim still in his remote location, lamenting his living conditions and longing to be near the house of God. Psalm 121 immediately follows, painting in beautiful brush strokes the image of a traveler on his journey. He looks at the hills in the distance, wondering and probably even fearing what might be on the other side. He anticipates the long, arduous journey ahead and, like all of us, wishes he could arrive in the blink of an eye rather than feel the effects of life on the road.

These are not the least of the reasons pilgrims sang their way to Jerusalem. Other scholars believe this psalm was also and perhaps especially intended for the departing journey after the feast concluded. Either way, the meaning is equally rich. In the inspired reassurance of the priest or leader in Psalm 121:3-8, you can assume that the pilgrim was experiencing all of the insecurities common to those traveling long distances in the open elements. We'll look at those more intimately tomorrow.

For now, center your attention on verse 2. What did the pilgrim call the Lord?

_____

The exact Hebrew phrase "Maker of heaven and earth" (v. 2) only occurs in the Hebrew Bible five times, each found in the psalms. Not coincidentally, three out of five uses are recorded in our Psalms of Ascent (Ps. 121:2; 124:8; 134:3). As I write this lesson, I'm on an airplane and trying to balance my laptop through some turbulence. Keith, Melissa, and I are on our way to South Africa where we'll do AIDS work and I'll speak at several conferences. I don't have a hard time piecing together why a traveler on an uncertain journey would want to remind himself that his God and his covenant LORD is the uncontested Maker of heaven and earth.

PRINCIPAL QUESTION

What connection do you see between taking an uncertain journey and wanting a reminder that your LORD is the uncontested Maker of heaven and earth?

_____

_____

A good friend of Melissa's will move to India in a few weeks to work in his company's foreign office for most of the next year. He will be one of the few Americans at his workplace. He shared with us that the idea that ours is a God who is with us has never meant more to him. In his aloneness and his remoteness, his God will be right there. Amid a life of passports, visas, and sometimes less than accommodating surroundings for Christians, I am so grateful that all the earth's turf is God's turf. We will never go anywhere God has abandoned precisely because He will never abandon us.

Now focus your gaze on verse 5, the very heart of the psalm. David G. Barker calls the first statement in this verse "the centerpoint for the entire psalm."[7]

Please star the first portion of Psalm 121:5 in both translations.

The second translation today is Hans-Joachim Kraus's in his commentary on psalms. He sought to translate the Hebrew as literally as possible. The two brief Hebrew words translated "Yahweh is your keeper" comprise the overarching message of the psalm. If we could see the original version, we'd see the phrase practically rises off the page in a ladder of words leading up to it and a ladder of equal stature descending down from it. You see, as Ceresko, an additional scholar, observed, 58 syllables (in Hebrew) precede the phrase translated "Yahweh is your keeper" and 58 syllables follow it.[8] That's one example of how carefully constructed many of the psalms are.

The central placement of the phrase "Yahweh is your keeper" was not enough for the inspired psalmist to make his point. He repeated forms of the word translated "keeper" numerous times, both prior to and following the phrase. Return to the text and place a check mark by each form of the word "protect" or "keep" in both versions. Each of those words comes from the root word transliterated *shamar*, meaning "to keep, guard … to preserve, protect; to watch."[9] Many of our English versions translate different words to make the reading easier and less repetitious.

For instance, in verses 7 and 8 alone, the New American Standard Bible translates the same Hebrew word with three different English terms. Locate and circle them:

"The LORD will protect you from all evil; He will keep your soul. The LORD will guard your going out and your coming in From this time forth and forever."

Interestingly, the psalmist who penned this song wasn't interested in varieties of words such as *protect, keep,* and *guard* to keep the singer engaged. He intended to hammer a point over and over again, repeating it until we got it: The LORD is your protector! The LORD will protect you from all harm! The LORD will protect your life! The LORD will protect your coming and going now and always!

Do you have any current need to have those truths hammered into your head, whether concerning your own life or another of God's children? If so, what is it?

PERSONAL QUESTION

_____

_____

What is God saying to you today? _____

_____

We'll continue our emphasis on this psalm tomorrow. But before we conclude today's lesson, please turn to Genesis 2:15.

What two purposes did God give man in the garden of Eden? (Circle two.)

Harvest it   Work it   Take care of it   Plow it   Measure it

The New International Version's phrase "take care of" and the Holman Christian Standard Bible's phrase "watch over" are each translated from that same Hebrew word *shamar.* God set Adam as caretaker over the garden, but God Himself was caretaker of Adam. As surely, thoughtfully, and purposefully as Adam cared for the ground God had given him, God cared for the man He'd formed with His own hands. Likewise, God is caretaker of you and of me. He tends to us. Watches over us. He has never entrusted that job to anyone else. At no time does God abdicate your guardianship to an angel alone, regardless of how mighty.

You and I are pilgrims here, sojourners on a path with twists and turns, with hills that obscure our view and incite us to fear what may lie on the other side. The earth is a minefield. Unseen enemies lurk in unexpected places. Simply put, it's scary here. Don't you think so?

If your answer is yes, what has most recently made you feel this way?

_____

_____

We need to know that God never takes His eyes off us as we travel the paths of this tumultuous planet. As I peck at this keyboard from my airplane seat, I hear a man close by gently snoring. I'm reminded that God never dozes off, even when for a time the air is smooth and the way is clear. He doesn't jolt awake when the earth rumbles beneath your feet. He is in perfect attendance to your every step.

We will make it to our destination in one piece. We will indeed "come to Mount Zion, to the heavenly Jerusalem, the city of the living God" (Heb. 12:22, NIV). No harm can befall us that will hinder our arrival, nor cloud surround us that will limit our view. Our God is the Lord, the Maker of heaven and earth. He owns the highways of both turfs.

Day Four
The Lord Is Your Shelter

Today we continue our focus on Psalm 121, the second step in our ascent. Please glance back at the text on day 3 and read either version of our psalm one more time. Let's return our thoughts to the question the pilgrim asked in the introduction to the psalm and make it our own. Beloved, where does your help come from?

If we've grown in the faith for long, we know the rhetorical answer to the question: The Lord our God, the Maker of heaven and earth, is our help. For just a moment, however, let's think in terms of human help. Most of the sojourners traveling many long miles back and forth to Jerusalem for the feasts were not traveling alone. Other Jews of the Diaspora accompanied them, ate with them, bunked with them, and sang the psalms with them. Scripture certainly supports the offer of human help.

What do the following Scriptures say about ways people can be of authentic help to one another?

Ecclesiastes 4:9-10 _____

_____

2 Corinthians 1:10-11 _____

_____

TODAY'S TREASURE

"The LORD protects you; the LORD is a shelter right by your side. The sun will not strike you by day, or the moon by night."
Psalm 121:5-6, HCSB

I don't know what I'd do without my fellow sojourners. A handful of girlfriends help me keep the faith, persevere through difficulty, love Keith more, and help me with the all-important things like whether my hair looks best shorter or longer. Whether that outfit is me. All kinds of girl stuff. God willing, I hope I am the same help to them.

How about you? Name a few people who are a tremendous help to you in your journey and how they help you.

_____

_____

So, with friends like ours, who needs divine help? Uh … let's see. That would be *every last one of us*. Why? Really meditate on this question for a moment.

Name specific ways God can help you that other people simply cannot.

PERSONAL QUESTION

_____

_____

As the pilgrim in Psalm 121 looked in the horizon and dreaded the long journey ahead, he was in good company and typical of the traveler to and from Jerusalem for the feasts. Like ours, his fellow sojourners could be great company and encouragement on the journey; but if an army rose against them or if the weather took a harrowing turn, they were just as human as he. And in just as much need.

Human help is wonderful, but it is always human. I'll give you an example. I fly so often that I'm hard to scare on an airplane. My children have always looked to me for reassurance when the ride gets bumpy. I smile at them and say, "We're just fine. It's nothing." Recently I was on a plane in such a storm that the young flight attendant looked like he'd seen a ghost. At first I did the nod and smile routine with him. Then the ride got so bad I quit smiling. Our need exceeded what man could do. Where did our help come from? Our help came from the Lord, Maker of heaven and earth.

Toward the beginning of yesterday's lesson, I asked you to search the psalm for indications that the lines were written from a traveler's perspective. Let's consider those now. Psalm 121:3 says, "He will not allow your foot to slip" (HCSB). Needless to say, the ancient traveler was making his journey primarily by foot. The terrain in the lands around Jerusalem could be treacherous. A twisted ankle or a broken foot could leave him stranded far from water. It could have been his ticket to the grave.

What does Jude 1:24 say Christ is able to do for us on our pilgrimage?

_____

"Your Protector will not slumber. Indeed, the Protector of Israel does not slumber or sleep."

Psalm 121:3-4, HCSB

Name a way He does that. _____

I don't care how long the flight, I have great difficulty sleeping on a plane. I think somewhere deep in my psyche, I believe a person ought to stay awake when suspended in midair. If I do happen to doze off, I certainly hope the pilot doesn't. Somebody had better stay awake. In essence, that was the psalmist's point. Most of the pilgrims making their way to Jerusalem traveled distances that necessitated sleeping somewhere on the way. Perhaps the wind whistled eerily around them or a wild dog howled in the distance. Scarier still, perhaps a bandit awaited their slumber so he could pounce on them in the night. When exhaustion overtook the travelers, yet they felt too insecure and exposed to sleep, they reassured themselves that Yahweh wouldn't blink an eye. Why? Because somebody had better stay awake. Another explanation for the reassurance that God never slumbers is intimated in 1 Kings 18:27.

What did Elijah suggest Baal, the god of the pagan enemies of Israel, might have been doing rather than coming to their rescue?

_____

Ancient pagan peoples commonly held the notion that gods slept or hibernated—even died, so to speak—during winter. The psalmist was assured his God was not like any other. "The Protector of Israel does not slumber or sleep" (Ps. 121:4, HCSB).

PRINCIPAL QUESTION

Psalm 121:5 says, "The LORD is a shelter right by your side" (HCSB). How does Psalm 91:4 depict the closeness of God's shelter?

_____

Psalm 121:6 says "The sun will not strike you by day, or the moon by night" (HCSB). Anyone who lives in a miserably hot climate can imagine the threat posed by a heatstroke to those traveling in a semi-desert terrain in the blazing sun. The reference to being moonstruck, however, is less common and much more intriguing. According to The Anchor Bible, "The notion that the moon beamed harmful influences was widespread in the ancient Near East."[10]

I can't wait to show you this: Compare Matthew 4:24 and 17:15. Note the references to "seizures" in the NIV or the HCSB. A commonly held belief in the ancient world was that seizures were caused by long or intense exposures to haunting effects of the moon. In fact, "moonstruck" is the literal rendering of the Greek word translated "seizures" in both verses.[11] The New American Standard Bible makes the connection perfectly for us in Matthew 17:15. "Lord, have mercy on my son, for he is a lunatic." Can you see the similarity of the words *lunar* and *lunatic*? The father believed the boy had been "moonstruck." Interesting, isn't it? Praise God, He protects us even where our superstitions mislead us.

Wait a minute. What about times our feet *have* slipped? Times we *have* been hurt on our journey? Where was God then? Did He promise something to Israel He did not promise to us? Not on your life. What was true of them in their physical pilgrimage is just as true of us in our spiritual journey. God always protects His children. Yes, *often* from the physical threats of the world around us, but *always* in the unseen realm where demons hiss and the gates of hell quake. Our feet do not slip in a world so real, so vivid, that ours is a shadow by comparison. The Lord lets no harm befall us in the world where the truest threats lie.

In Matthew 10:28, Christ said, "Don't fear those who kill the body but are not able to kill the soul" (HCSB). I'm human just like you, and these words can seem like small consolation as we travel this dangerous turf. But when our eyes are truly opened and we see all the ways hell rose against us, the Devil wanted us, and God hid us in the shadow of His wings, we will drop on our knees and worship the Maker of heaven and earth.

I have so enjoyed studying this glorious psalm with you. We've *said it*, *worked it*, and now it's time for us to conclude by *praying it*. Please transform Psalm 121 into your own prayer below. While it's fresh on your mind, don't forget to turn to the back of your workbook and write a brief sentence on your stair graphic describing what the psalm has taught you. Also begin actively memorizing the psalm in the Holman Christian Standard Bible. Enough instructions! Great job, Beloved!

My Psalm 121

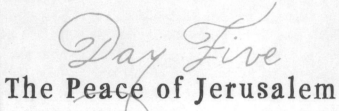

The Peace of Jerusalem

We begin our third step in our Psalms of Ascent today. One of the things I love about God is that He sees progress even in our small steps. He sees infinitely into the past and the future, so He knows when an inch we've taken is going to turn into a mile.

As I write, my first grandchild, our beloved Jackson, is six months old. My daughter Amanda and son-in-law Curt have invited Keith and me to be part of every inch of progress he's made. I was there the first time he focused on his young mother's face and we could see him studying her features carefully. I know the first time he smiled on purpose, and oh, what inexpressible joy! Amanda called me the morning after he first slept through the night. I know exactly when he rolled from his stomach to his back and from his back to his stomach. God be praised, I know the moment he undoubtedly recognized his grand-dad and me and grinned at us with familial affection.

I don't sit over Jackson impatiently and wish he were suddenly grown. I celebrate every step he takes. Why do we think our Heavenly Father, who designed our bodies, souls, and spirits to operate just as they do, would be any different? No, God doesn't enjoy a child's stubborn unwillingness to grow up any more than I'd enjoy Jackson still crawling at six years of age. But I am convinced God thoroughly relishes every hint of maturity even if we feel as if we're not making progress.

Almost every time I point out an area to my young adult daughters where I can really see they've grown spiritually, they'll say something like, "Thanks, Mom. I needed to hear that. Sometimes I wonder if I'm getting anywhere at all." Do you feel that way sometimes? Let me start your day of homework with some encouragement.

What does Isaiah 55:10-11 say about God's Word? _____

_____

As you study Scripture, God is accomplishing something in you. As long as you keep your heart exposed to it and don't compartmentalize everything you're learning in your head alone, you can't help but make some level of progress as you give this kind of time to study. Just think what can happen when we become intentional about it!

OK, let's get to our third Psalm of Ascent. Quick review: What three approaches are we going to take? _____ it, _____ it, and at the conclusion of our next day of study, we'll _____ it. Proceed with the first two approaches now:

TODAY'S TREASURE

"Pray for the peace of Jerusalem. 'May those who love you prosper.'"
Psalm 122:6, HCSB

PSALM 122 *(HCSB)*

A Prayer for Jerusalem
A Davidic song of ascents.

1 I rejoiced with those who said to me,
 "Let us go to the house of the LORD."
2 Our feet are standing
 within your gates, Jerusalem—
3 Jerusalem, built as a city [should be],
 solidly joined together,
4 where the tribes, the tribes of the LORD, go up
 to give thanks to the name of the LORD.
 (This is an ordinance for Israel.)
5 There, thrones for judgment are placed,
 thrones of the house of David.
6 Pray for the peace of Jerusalem:
 "May those who love you prosper;
7 may there be peace within your walls,
 prosperity within your fortresses."
8 Because of my brothers and friends,
 I will say, "Peace be with you."
9 Because of the house of the LORD our God,
 I will seek your good.

PSALM 122 *(NLT)*

A song for the ascent to Jerusalem.
A psalm of David.

1 I was glad when they said to me, "Let us go to the
 house of the LORD."
2 And now we are standing here inside your gates,
 O Jerusalem.
3 Jerusalem is a well-built city, knit together as a single
 unit.
4 All the people of Israel—the LORD's people— make
 their pilgrimage here. They come to give thanks to
 the name of the LORD as the law requires.
5 Here stand the thrones where judgment is given,
 the thrones of the dynasty of David.
6 Pray for the peace of Jerusalem. May all who love
 this city prosper.
7 O Jerusalem, may there be peace within your walls
 and prosperity in your palaces.
8 For the sake of my family and friends, I will say,
 "Peace be with you."
9 For the sake of the house of the LORD our God,
 I will seek what is best for you, O Jerusalem.

Did you catch the progression of the pilgrimage? Glance back over the wording.
Where was the psalmist when these words fell from his lips? (See v. 2.)

Reflect on the two previous psalms. Recall with me that the first Psalm of Ascent seemed to position the pilgrim in an alien land—in Meshech and "among the tents of Kedar." Psalm 121 pictured the pilgrim on his journey, gazing at the hills before him ("where does my help come from?"), enduring harsh elements ("the sun will not harm you by day") and dreading the dark of night ("nor the moon by night").

In the third psalm he stands with weary feet and a glad heart on the soil of his destination. We celebrate his arrival within the gates of the holy city, the traveler's long-sought and beloved Jerusalem. Is anything quite like getting where we're going and not being disappointed? Beloved, if you and I only knew what we have ahead, our hearts would race and our pace would quicken.

The primary focus of Psalm 122 is the city itself. Indeed, much of the song is a play on the word *Jerusalem*—"yeru" meaning "city" and "salem" meaning "peace."[12] I can't wait until heaven when I'm counting on all of us being able to speak multiple languages and, above all, Hebrew! We miss so much of the art and beauty of poetic Scripture by not hearing it in the original language. If we could read Psalm 122 aloud in Hebrew, we'd hear what *Word Biblical Commentary* calls a "sixfold alliteration" playing on the name Jerusalem in verses 6-8.[13] My younger daughter, Melissa, has done her postgraduate work in biblical languages so she showed me the similarity of the words and read it aloud so I could hear the repeated sounds. To explain it as simply as possible, six words in Psalm 122:6-8 carry the "sh" sound prominent in the more familiar Hebrew word *shalom*. I'll show you how it worked by choosing another sound and writing my own as an example: Give praise to the God of glory whose greatness brings grandeur and whose goodness brings gladness.

Now, you try it. Come on! Don't be a stick in the mud. There's a psalmist in all of us. Write a line or two of praise that repeats one sound:

_____

_____

You'll be relieved to know that I won't ask you to write a tune to go with it, but imagine how much beauty the music added to the alliteration. Truly, the psalms are masterpieces.

Once again, what does the word Jerusalem *mean?* _____

Look back at the psalm. How did the psalmist describe Jerusalem?

_____

_____

No other city is like Jerusalem. It beckons sojourners like no other land, and like no other place I've ever been, it lends a strange sense of "home" even to the visitor casting her first glance. Kay Arthur once told me that the more you go to Jerusalem, the more you want to go. I've found that to be true. I felt the spiritual draw the first time I went, but after the second time, I departed with a sense of urgency that I must go again and again. If you and I were gathered to the east of the city on the Mount of Olives like I wish we were right now, we'd obviously see a different kind of city than the one that captured the psalmist's attention. At least one characteristic hasn't changed, however. Jerusalem is still a city "that is closely compacted together" (Ps. 122:3, NIV).

I love the visual in the New Living Translation. *How does it say the same thing?*

_____

The close-knit appearance of modern Jerusalem may make it look like one large unit, but in this case, looks are deceiving. Ironically, peace is a rarity in the "City of Peace." Even if days pass without violence, the tension is practically palpable within the closely compacted city between its Jewish, Muslim, and Christian inhabitants. One day I passed an Israeli soldier standing guard with an automatic weapon, and I told my guide that he made me nervous. I'll never forget my guide's response: "Ah, to the contrary, Miss Beth. He is there to make you feel safe." I tried to buy into that mentality, but at times I can't help feeling a little insecure. Still, the trek is worth it to me.

Many Christians hope to go to Jerusalem someday "when things settle down over there." And understandably so. Have you ever noticed that things rarely settle down over there? The ancient words of the psalmist cry out with fervor to us today: "Pray for the peace of Jerusalem!"

I love Jewish people, and God continues to flourish a deep affection for their beloved city, Jerusalem, in my heart. I yearn to see peace in their land, but according to Scripture certain things must happen before peace will reign within her walls.

What is the ultimate reason peace eludes the holy city according to Luke 19:41-44?

_____

Read Ephesians 2:11-22 carefully. What parallels apply to what we're learning in today's lesson? Be sure and note any talk of "foreigners" or "aliens."

PRINCIPAL QUESTION

_____

What is Christ called in Ephesians 2:14? _____

With this added insight into true peace from the New Testament, would you conclude today's lesson by writing a prayer below for the peace of Jerusalem?

_____

_____

_____

_____

May those who love Jerusalem prosper (Ps. 122:6).

viewer guide

Where Will My Help Come From?

If you are participating in the homework and were able to complete week 1, by this time you have placed both feet on the first two psalms and one foot on the third. You also know by now that Psalm 121 will comprise our memory work for this six-week series. In today's session you and I will focus on the psalms as songs. To grasp more of the significance, we will view the element of song beyond the psalms.

1. Song originated with God and accompanied _____ (*Job 38:7*).

In Scripture singing is attributed to both _____ the _____

and _____ the _____

(*Zeph. 3:17, NIV; Matt. 26:30, HCSB; Heb. 2:10-12*).

2. _____ and _____ can be expressed through

song in ways _____ words can never _____

(*Jas. 5:13; Ps. 13; Hos. 2:14-15*).

3. A song greatly enhances the _____ of the human mind to

_____ (*Deut. 31:19-22*).

4. See Ezekiel 33:30-32. We can think a song is _____ and

memorize its words yet remain completely _____

by what it says. Consider the relevance of Paul's words in 1 Corinthians 14:15 in

our present context: "I will sing with my _____, but I will also sing

with my _____."

5. A song can _____ our entire perspective (*Acts 16:24-26*).

A song can also greatly _____ the heart of _____.

6. See Revelation 5:13. In the *New International Commentary of the New Testament*,

Robert Mounce describes this scene as "the adoration of the entire

_____ _____." In ways beyond our comprehension,

the gift of song is not limited to _____ and _____.

Day One: Our Own House,
Our Own City
Day Two: The One Enthroned
Day Three: Much Contempt
Day Four: If The Lord
Had Not
Day Five: Praise the Lord

Principal Questions

1. What were Paul's feelings toward the believers in Philippi (Phil. 1:3-8)?

2. What do you consider to be the theme of Psalm 123?

3. How would you define *disrespect*?

4. With what metaphors does Psalm 124 describe the peril that surrounds God's people?

5. With what three historical situations were the Psalms of Ascent associated?

Day One

Our Own House, Our Own City

As we begin our second week, we place both feet on the third step of our ascent. Please read either of the translations of Psalm 122 in the previous lesson to refresh your memory. When you've read it, check here: _____

On week 1, day 5 we viewed Psalm 122 in a more literal context. Today we are going to draw parallels between the rich lines of the song and our own lives. Each of us has a different heritage God uses to fashion us into the servants He wants us to be. My friend, Jolinda, pours out her life for those who are HIV positive in South Africa. An avowed atheist until five years ago, she met God and instantly enrolled in seminary. As I watched her minister in her unique environment, I marveled over God's brilliance to choose not only Jolinda's exact personality but also her exact past. The fact that she was not raised in a highly religious culture, I believe, works in significant ways in her favor. She doesn't speak Christian-ese so fluently that individuals she works with can't understand her explanations.

On the other hand, you may be like me. I was on the cradle roll at church and learned to toddle on heel-marked linoleum strewn with brightly colored blocks and oversized puzzle pieces. By the time I could sit in a miniature chair and hear a child-size Bible story, I already bore the signs of sexual abuse. How I still believed in the goodness of the God my Sunday School teachers taught about remains a mystery to me. I am so grateful to God for the grace to believe amid the madness.

Our teachers encouraged us to learn short Bible verses long before we could read. *Today's Treasure* is dear to me because it is one of the first verses I ever memorized. Glance at it again. The corresponding picture my teachers displayed with the verse had a young mom and dad and several children walking together on the sidewalk toward their church, each smiling ear to ear. (Perhaps that was the one lone Sunday they didn't have a fight in the car on the way.) A more literal visual for the psalm would have been a picture of Jews climbing the steps to the temple in ancient Jerusalem, but four-year-olds would have had difficulty relating.

While the trek to our churches bears few true parallels to the pilgrimage to Israel's central location for worship, let's not be so academic that we miss the sentiment. Consider an explanation from *Word Biblical Commentary*. It tells us Psalm 122 "like Psalm 84, regards Jerusalem with a pilgrim's warmth of religious emotion rather than with depth of theological learning."[1] Today I wonder if you'd be sappy enough to enter into "a pilgrim's warmth of spiritual emotion" with me. The apostle Paul was a theologian if you've ever imagined one, but his cup overflowed with sentiment when he spoke of local groups of believers who'd become so dear to him.

TODAY'S TREASURE

"I rejoiced with those who said to me, 'Let us go to the house of the LORD.' "
Psalm 122:1, HCSB

What were Paul's feelings toward the believers in Philippi (Phil. 1:3-8)?

_____

_____

I love church. God has made it a refuge for me since childhood. I've never attended a perfect one and would have ruined it if I had. No, I don't always feel like going, and something monumental doesn't happen every time I go. Still, I am blessed and built up in spirit enough to tackle another vicious Monday morning. Nothing makes me happier than hearing from brand-new believers who have come to know Jesus through their small group. If you're among them, I hope you've had time enough in your walk with God to get plugged into a local body of believers. If you haven't, please don't let the dust settle, but in the meantime answer the following questions in terms of what you hope to *find* in a local church and *bring* to a local church.

Accepting that no fellowship of believers is perfect, what are a few things you really love about yours?

_____

_____

Name some people you look forward to seeing each time you go and explain why.

_____

_____

One of the things I like best about a functioning church home is the invitation to form relationships with people I might otherwise miss—with people altogether different than me. For instance, I have a whole set of girlfriends ranging from ages 7-12 that I talk to every Sunday and several of them—via text message—during the week.

What about you? Describe a few relationships you have at church that you wouldn't have anywhere else.

_____

_____

Here's the bottom line according to *Today's Treasure*. Are you glad when someone says to you, "Let's go to the house of the LORD"?

While few people are enthusiastically anxious to roll out of bed every Sunday after an exhausting week, do you ordinarily look forward to going to church?

Almost never   Sometimes   Usually   Almost always

If your answer is "almost never" or perhaps even "sometimes," this lesson may be more important for you. Church is a huge part of the believer's life—as big as your workplace or the neighborhood where you live. I can confidently say that God is not without an opinion about how you invest your life in a spiritual community. Ask Him about what He wants you to do about church. If you aren't looking forward to church, maybe He can show you what you can do to change the situation. Sometimes He requires a change in us. Sometimes the Father even uses our dissatisfaction to show us He wants to move us to another ministry in another place.

Note how the psalmist began with a focus on the temple or "house of the LORD" and then widened his focus to the city surrounding it. We're going to follow suit. In Jeremiah 29 God gave profound and timely instructions through His prophet to the people of God in Babylonian captivity. In some respects you and I may think of ourselves as exiles, not because of disobedience to God but because we are citizens of heaven (Phil. 3:20) with ankles chained to earth.

What was God's essential point to the exiles in Babylon (Jer. 29:4-7)?

_____

How can we draw a parallel between verse 7, Psalm 122:6, and our own cities?

_____

In our previous lesson we talked about how God fits us with our personalities, uses our pasts, and plants our feet in places to fashion us into servants who can do some good. I was raised in a small Arkansas town where I attended ninth grade with most of the same people I sat next to in kindergarten. Smack in the middle of my high school years my parents packed my little brother and me in the old Buick and headed to Houston, Texas—the biggest city in the South. Talk about life interrupted!

Many years passed before I saw God's wisdom in exposing me widely to both environments. Because all my formative years were in a smaller town, I am very comfortable serving in those environments. I've seen life from the stands of the local football field where everybody cheers for one high school team. From that smaller environment, I've also seen life from the neighborhood street corner where everybody not only knows your name but also your business. Good, bad, and the ugly—I hated to let it go. I've done life since then from six lanes of crowded overpasses where we honk a crude brand of Morse code to one another.

Let's face it. Most of us have a love-hate relationship with the places we've gotten our mail, but God intended to use every stop to equip us as servants. You have been assigned to your town or your city, and equally, it has been assigned to you. You may feel like an exile within its city limits, but just as God spoke through the prophet Jeremiah, He wants to prosper you there. His method may not be through all your city can do to edify and serve you. It may be what you can do to build up your city—one neighbor, one teacher, one trash collector at a time. Please give these two questions some thought:

How is God using your town or city to equip you to be a humble servant?

_____

How is God using you in your town or city? _____

_____

Remember, you don't have to be on the school board or in city government for God to use you. He ministers to cities just as readily by ministering to neighbors. The point is to understand that we've been called by God's purpose to the places we live.

We've practiced our first two approaches to Psalm 122. We've said it and worked it. Now as you "pray it," update the psalm to reflect your own church and city. Speak blessing over your city as the psalmist did. Then fill in your stair graphic.

Fabulous job today, Dear One. Keep stepping up.

My Psalm 122

Day Two
The One Enthroned

Today we place our right foot on the fourth stair as we study Psalm 123. I'm anxious to discuss the material with you and don't want to waste a moment getting started. I so hope you're still taking your place on your face and having some breakthroughs with God you might not otherwise have.

Go ahead and plunge into both of the following translations of Psalm 123: *Say it;* then *work it.* Toward the conclusion of day 3, we'll *pray it.*

PSALM 123 (HCSB)

1 I lift my eyes to You,
  the One enthroned in heaven.
2 Like a servant's eyes on His master's hand,
  like a servant girl's eyes on her mistress's hand,
  so our eyes are on the LORD our God
  until He shows us favor.
3 Show us favor, LORD, show us favor,
  for we've had more than enough contempt.
4 We've had more than enough
  scorn from the arrogant
  and contempt from the proud.

PSALM 123 (The Amplified Bible)

1 Unto You do I lift up my eyes,
  O You Who are enthroned in heaven.
2 Behold, as the eyes of servants
  look to the hand of their master,
  and as the eyes of a maid
  to the hand of her mistress,
  so our eyes look to the Lord our God,
  until He has mercy and loving-kindness for us.
3 Have mercy on us,
  O Lord, have mercy on and loving-kindness for us,
  for we are exceedingly satiated with contempt.
4 Our life is exceedingly filled with the scorning
  and scoffing of those who are at ease
  and with the contempt of the proud
  (irresponsible tyrants who disregard God's law).

PRINCIPAL QUESTION

In one phrase or sentence, what do you consider to be the theme of Psalm 123?

Today consider verses 1 and 2 of this rich psalm. Psalm 123 falls into the genre of songs of lament, but the focus is God Himself. The first question is this: Where are we looking? Right now in the challenge that surrounds me and all that busies me or injures me, where am *I* looking? Where are *my* attentions focused?

Without a hint of condemnation, let's plunge beneath our rote spiritual answers to what's true. When every natural instinct begs us to stare wide-eyed in the face of our circumstances, demands, oppressors, and false saviors, what—or who—ultimately wins our focus? These questions are vital because much of our soul's basic welfare is wrapped up in our answers.

I'd like to suggest that an entire chain reaction begins with our eyes and ultimately affects our hearts, souls, and minds. *Where we look*—where we genuinely fasten our gaze—amid continual life challenges has a tremendous impact on *how we feel*.

Have you discovered a strong relationship in the concept of the statement Where I look impacts How I feel? *If so, how? Try to get specific.*

_____

_____

I am convinced that one reason *where we look* has such an impact on *how we feel* is because where we look is also primarily where we listen. Stay with me here and let me see if I can illustrate the point in Scripture.

Read Acts 3:1-7. This is a perfect time to take a glance at your temple diagram. Describe where this encounter between Peter, John, and the beggar took place.

_____

Now look carefully at Acts 3:4. What did Peter say to the beggar? _____

Complete Acts 3:5: "So the man _____ _____ _____ _____,
expecting to get something from them" (NIV).

Verse 3 tells us the man "saw" them and asked them for money but obviously with half a glance, half a heart, and probably less than half an expectation. Until Peter demanded his attention, the crippled man simply did what he did "every day" (v. 2). By reading verse 5 carefully, you'll see that the man gave Peter and John neither his full attention nor his great expectation until he looked straight at them.

Therefore, he *looked*, which caused him to more effectively *listen*, which in turn altered his *feelings*, manifesting in a change in his *expectation*. Needless to say, the beggar got far more than he expected, but until he "gave them his attention" he had no real expectation of anything out of the ordinary.

Look at each of the following phrases and the impact they have on one another.

Where I look $\longrightarrow$ What I hear $\longrightarrow$ What I feel $\longrightarrow$ What I expect

How could the same concepts in your approach to God impact your life?

_____

_____

Like the crippled man begging at the Gate Beautiful, we can rise up early in the morning and keep our routine prayer time, say all the right things yet remain so focused on our circumstances that nothing ever changes. Let's hear our wonderful God say to us today, "Look at Me!" How worthy is He of our gaze?

How is God described in Psalm 123:1? _____

During staff prayer time a few days ago I told my coworkers at Living Proof Ministries that I never want us to get so "spiritual" and think ourselves so mature that we lose touch with the common questions and concerns of the masses that we've been called to serve. Many people secretly wonder, *Who is God that we should seek Him first?* Or in today's lesson's terminology, "Who is God that we should look to Him alone?" Certainly people struggle with the question, "Who is God that we should obey Him as servants?" Simply put, who does God think He is?

While respectful men and women may be scared to voice such questions aloud, Scripture is not the least bit reluctant to offer answers. God tells us exactly who He thinks—and knows—He is. He does not call us to worship and serve ignorantly and stumble before Him blindly. Students of sound biblical theology will discover that Christianity is a thinking and reasoning person's belief system.

Psalm 123:1 intimates that one chief reason God is worthy of being the One to whom we lift our eyes and fix our focus is because He is "enthroned in heaven." Let's take this one description of God and see what else the psalms have to say about it.

List what the following psalms tell us about God's enthronement.

Psalm 22:3-4 _____

Psalm 29:10 _____

Psalm 99:1 _____

Psalm 113:4-6 _____

Circle the key word in this term: enthroned.

Enthroned on high and between the cherubim, God rules over the entire universe. You can't be "enthroned" without a "throne" (the key word). Like the 24 elders pictured in Revelation 4:10-11, ultimately every other crown bearer will "fall down before him who sits on the throne, and worship him who lives for ever and ever." They will "lay their crowns before the throne and say: 'You are worthy, our Lord and God.'"

Isaiah 1:18 says, "'Come now, let us reason together,' says the LORD."

Nothing operates outside God's sovereign rule, including any prince or principality of earth or air, and yet God is the ultimate exception to the saying that "absolute power corrupts absolutely." Psalm 22:3 (NIV) tells us, God is "enthroned as the Holy One." He cannot be unholy in any dimension of His authority.

These are a few of the reasons why He is worthy of our fixed attentions. These are also a few of the reasons why everything else will downsize into its proper place when we look to God alone. Just as God is enthroned over the flood, He is enthroned over everything that troubles you.

What is one of your foremost concerns? (Complete the following sentence.)
Lord, You are the Holy One and You are alertly and lovingly enthroned over

---

God calls us to look to Him, seek and find in Him, but He wants us to approach on His terms based on who He really is. Not as we think we'd like to make Him. Eugene Peterson frames it beautifully. Reflect on his words in the next two paragraphs.

> "We are not presented with a functional god who will help us out of jams or an entertainment god who will lighten our tedious hours. We are presented with the God of exodus and Easter, the God of Sinai and Calvary. If we want to understand God, we must do it on his terms. If we want to see God the way he really is, we must look to the place of authority—to Scripture and to Jesus Christ.
>
> "And do we really want it any other way? I don't think so. We would very soon become contemptuous of a god whom we could figure out like a puzzle or learn to use like a tool. No, if God is worth our attention at all, he must be a God we can look up to—a God we *must* look up to … The moment we look up to God (and not over at him, or down on him) we are in the posture of servitude."[2]

Peterson doesn't mean God can't or won't get us out of jams. But if that's all we make of Him, we've missed the true enormity of God. Think about what Peterson said about figuring God out like a puzzle. Consider afresh that God was just as intentional about what He didn't tell us in Scripture as what He did. You might say that what is missing and unexplained on the pages of Scripture is in some ways just as inspired as what you find in ink. Who else is so brilliant, so multidimensional and gloriously mysterious that you could spend your entire life studying and never grasp His vastness?

Ask yourself two questions as I pose the same ones to myself, and let's be honest in our personal assessment.

What do you think you'd do if you thought you had God completely figured out?

What if you could learn to use God like a tool and get anything you wanted?

_____

God is so wise, isn't He? As wise in what He's hidden as in what He's disclosed. As wise in what He doesn't do as what He does. Make no mistake. He is all-powerful and ever willing to use that power on behalf of His children. We see glimpses of this accessibility intimated in Psalm 123. Consider comments from *The Eerdmans Critical Commentary* of this brief psalm of ascent.

> "The singer affirms his total devotion to the Lord, and he wants to obtain a vision of the divine presence. … His eyes are fixed on God's hands. To lift up the eyes is a gesture of deep longing. While God is enthroned in the heavens—a sign of his kingship—his transcendence is not inaccessible. God's crowd of helpers, like royal attendants, wait for a single hint before going into action."[3]

How do you respond to these thoughts?_____

_____

_____

"I lift my eyes to You, the One enthroned in heaven."

Psalm 123:1, HCSB

After the psalmist set his gaze on the One enthroned in heaven in Psalm 123:1, he affirmed his position as His servant in verse 2. Did you notice the contrast between the plural reference to "slaves" (in this context men only) and their master and the singular reference to the "maid" and her mistress? John Eaton explains, "The male servants are more numerous for the work in the fields; the single maid assisting her mistress in the house may have come with her at the marriage."[4]

I have no idea how a man would look at the reference to his role as servant in this verse, but as a woman I am tendered by the image of just one feminine servant sitting at the hand of her master (rather than a mistress, of course, as we draw our own parallel). I don't want to make too much of it because the psalm is not making much of it; but something in every woman longs to see herself for just a moment as the only one at her dearest love's hand. Take that opportunity, Dear One, right this moment.

Yes, you and I have the joy of laboring beside many wonderful fellow servants, but perhaps today your feminine heart needs to see itself—all by yourself—right there at the hand of your Master, Jesus. Yes, you look to Him as do many others around you. But I think it might be all right today if you also imagined that there are times when He only has eyes for you. Somehow in His limitless capacity to love, nurture, and watch over us, Christ can attend to each of us as if we are the only one in the world.

Take a moment today as you conclude and sense Christ's gaze upon *you*, His Beloved.

Day Three
Much Contempt

Today we plant both feet firmly on Psalm 123. In our last lesson I received a fresh instruction from God about becoming more deliberate in setting my gaze. If I have low expectations, skewed feelings, and impaired spiritual hearing, my eyes are either looking in at myself or out at people and circumstances. I hope you're getting some insight from the words of the psalmist too. God wants our eyes fixed upward like someone down on her knees at His feet.

We tend to focus on the most obvious. God wants to equip us with a vision that sees higher, deeper, and broader than our physical realities. According to Ephesians 1:18, we can have the eyes of our hearts enlightened. Perhaps that's the essence of true vision: seeing clearest of all with the eyes of our hearts.

On day 2 we focused on Psalm 123:1-2. Today we turn our attentions to verses 3 and 4. Please turn back to your previous lesson, choose one translation of Psalm 123 and read it in its entirety.

As we zero in on the second half of the psalm, what specific reason did the psalmist give for requesting mercy? Choose one answer.

_____ *They had sinned grievously.*   _____ *They were in physical danger.*
_____ *They were in captivity.*   _____ *They had endured much contempt.*

I can't imagine we'll have any trouble relating to the psalmist today. Scripture may use different wording than our day-to-day vocabulary, but the actions and the feelings described in Psalm 123 are thoroughly familiar to us. The Hebrew term translated "contempt" comes from a root that means "to disrespect."[5]

Surely we all know what it's like to be treated disrespectfully. Meditate on the word for a moment. Offer your own general definition of disrespect; then give two examples.

Definition: _____

_____

Examples:

1. _____

2. _____

Disrespect is not the same as disagreement. We can strongly disagree and still treat people with respect.

Disrespect is not the same as disagreement. We can strongly disagree and still treat people with respect. Disrespect devalues them. We can disrespect people in the way we talk to them or refuse to talk to them. Someone can say all the right things yet have a tone, expression, or manner that exudes disrespect. We can be disrespectful in the way we look at the person talking to us or even more disrespectful in our refusal to look. Disrespect is treating someone as inferior or simply not worth the courtesy. In a nutshell, it is the disregard of innate human value.

I'll never forget the time Keith, our daughters, and I were on a subway in Paris. Our girls were older teenagers at the time, and some of the men standing around them gawked inappropriately at them. Keith cleared his throat, stared the offenders down, and did everything possible to make sure they knew he was the father of those two girls. Still, they persisted. Keith was so furious I was afraid somebody was going to get off that train with a black eye. He could not fathom such disrespect. Later he said, "They kept staring at the girls with me, their father, standing right next to them. Those men could also clearly see that I disapproved. How much gall does that take?" Thankfully, we got off the subway in the nick of time before anybody got hurt. Trust me when I tell you the problem was not a language barrier. It was disrespect.

Hopefully by now all sorts of examples of disrespect are swimming around in your head. Picture that they are neither isolated occurrences nor relatively benign expressions of disrespect. Picture them constant and blatant. That's the kind of disrespect the psalmist is talking about.

Fill in the following blank according to the Amplified Bible's version of Psalm 123:3 in your previous lesson: "Have mercy on us, O Lord, have mercy on and loving-kindness for us, for we are …

In our words? *We're up to here with it! We've had it!* Ever felt that way? Boy, I have! I don't doubt I've caused others to feel that way at times. Today's lesson is for times when we are at the end of our rope with a situation and yet it's not a simple matter of just walking away. Maybe we've nearly had it with a situation at work, yet we want that job. Maybe we've nearly had it with a situation at home, yet we want that marriage. Maybe we're at our wits end with a friendship, but we hate to let the whole thing go over one frustrating area. On the other hand, maybe we'd really like to walk away, but it simply isn't God's will and we're trying to be obedient.

We can relate to the writer of Psalm 123 every time we want to echo the words of verse 4 (HCSB): *I've had more than enough.* Not just enough, Lord. *More than enough.* Think about when you've felt that way. Was one of the major issues a feeling that you were being disrespected? When a wife continues to catch a husband with pornography, along with the obvious sense of betrayal, doesn't she also battle an overwhelming sense that she's not respected? When a husband continues to be belittled by his wife, pressured to *make* more or *be* more, isn't she treating him with disrespect?

*List another example when some expression of ongoing disrespect can lead
a person to feel like he or she has had "more than enough."*

_____

Psalm 123 is ink to the page for such a time as this. It stands as permission to come to
God—not arrogantly or with our own expression of disrespect but on our knees—as
a servant looks to her master. That's the perfect posture for saying, "Lord, I've got to
have Your help. I've had more than enough. I'm not going to make it in this situation
without You."

Now let's look at a very specific expression of disrespect that I think is best worded
in Psalm 123:4 by the NIV. "We have endured much *ridicule*" (emphasis mine). At first
glance, ridicule seems relatively innocuous. It seems the lesser of contemptuous evils
and something we ought to be able to take. A steady stream of ridicule, however, can
become terribly oppressive. Ridicule can take us on a trip to "more than enough" in
record time. Let's face it. All of us are quirky. Goodness knows, I provide ample fodder
for someone to make fun of me. As you might imagine, my enthusiasm has been
mocked a few times, and let's not even talk about my hair!

How about you? For what could others fairly readily ridicule you?

_____

We're odd enough on our own. Add Christianity to the mix and we're a peculiar
people indeed. You may be ridiculed at work or at school for having what some of
your coworkers consider an archaic set of values. A friend of mine told me that in
college she tried to get rid of her virginity as quickly as she could because people
made so much fun of her. Or in a totally different vein, unbelieving friends or family
members may ridicule you for what another Christian said or did in public. I've
been there. A constant dose of ridicule can be hard to swallow. It's difficult enough
for mature adults, but I'd like to suggest that ridicule can be toxic for children and
adolescents. Even deadly.

Most of us doing this Bible study are women, and although many of us are not
actively parenting within our homes, we find ourselves in all sorts of positions where
we may see a young person being bullied. Schoolteachers, Sunday School teachers,
principals, counselors, and nurses may see all sorts of evidences that a child is being
harshly ridiculed. A neighbor can take note of something harmful happening to a
child on the street or at the bus stop. We can't just take the child's word for it if he
says it doesn't bother him. His actions and his demeanor speak louder than his words.
Sometimes a child is so desperate to be liked and accepted that he'll put up with
anything. What should we do? Go back to our knees like servants at the hands of our
master and seek God's mercy and the revelation of His wisdom. The psalmists offer
all sorts of ways we can relate personally, but sometimes we're more readily reminded
of what someone else is enduring.

Have you ever seen a person harshly ridiculed? If so, how?

_____

What did you do or wish you could have done? _____

_____

From now on, we can see something like you described as a perfect opportunity to turn the words of Psalm 123 into intercession. On another person's behalf, we can tell God that we think he or she has had *more than enough*. While we're at it, we can ask Him if we are meant to take any kind of action. Be sure to test what you think you've heard by lining it up against the Word, and in particularly volatile matters, consider seeking the counsel of someone you trust. If God wills you to action, have the courage to do what He leads.

In conclusion, let's look at the wider picture once again. At one time or another all of us have been targets of disrespect or ridicule. Furthermore, we who belong to God through Christ Jesus are all regarded as children to God. When His beloved child receives this kind of mistreatment, she is not without recourse. She has an Advocate. Tell God what is happening. Get the weight of it off your chest. See yourself as He sees you and picture Him standing between you and the person mistreating you. Ask for wisdom to know what to do. Also have the courage to ask God if you're unknowingly doing anything to invite it. When I was young, I had a victim mentality that seemed to issue one invitation after another for someone to hurt me. Needless to say, I had a string of people who were more than willing to RSVP. Other times the problem resides solely in another person and we're doing nothing to invite it. God can show us the difference.

Above all, when we've had *more than enough* disrespect or ridicule, we need to do exactly what the inspired writer of Psalm 123 did: feverishly seek God's mercy. When we ask for God's mercy according to the definition of the Hebrew word translated *mercy* in Psalm 123, we're asking for God's favor, for His kindness, and His grace. In fact, *grace* is probably the closest New Testament equivalent to the Old Testament term translated "mercy" in this psalm.[6]

Why would the favor, kindness, and grace of God be effective remedies when we feel disrespected or ridiculed? Explain briefly.

_____

_____

Eerdmans Critical Commentary offers these statements concerning the pleas for mercy in Psalm 123. "A repeated supplication, 'Have mercy upon us' could be rendered 'Grace us!' The Hebrew verb means not only 'have mercy' but also, in archaic English, 'Grace us,' that is to say 'Transform us into thy treasure,' make us receive this divine quality that incorporates us into thy closest family."[7]

Beloved, according to God's precious Word, if you belong to Jesus Christ, you've already been transformed into God's treasure. You are already the closest of family. Romans 8:17 says, "If we are children, then we are heirs—heirs of God and co-heirs with Christ." As we fellowship in His sufferings, we will inevitably experience various expressions of disrespect and ridicule from time to time, but we are not helpless. We know where to go. And we're going to go there today.

Glance back over your two lessons on Psalm 123. Think about some of the things God has revealed to you and unearthed in you; then speak to Him from those very depths as you write your own rendition of Psalm 123. If it simply doesn't apply to you right now, without using his or her name, pray it for someone else you know who is treated with disrespect. Don't forget to fill in your stair graphic for Psalm 123 with a phrase describing what you most want to take with you from this psalm.

My Psalm 123

If the Lord Had Not

TREASURE

"If the LORD had not been on our side when men attacked us, then they would have swallowed us alive."
Psalm 124:2-3, HCSB

We've arrived at the fifth step in our ascent to the next level with God. I am already completely captivated by the material. I've begun to talk to God about things I've never thought to address with Him before. My deep hope is that God is captivating you too. He delights in your pursuit of Him, Precious One. Don't think for a moment He is inattentive as you throw open your Bible and seek to hear His voice amid so many voices competing for your attention. God is ready and waiting for you every time you approach Him and He promised if you seek Him and His righteousness first, He will add everything else of value to your life (see Matt. 6:33). Let's put our right foot on the next step. Please read both translations of Psalm 124 and apply your first two approaches.

PSALM 124:1-8 (HCSB)

1 If the LORD had not been on our side—
   let Israel say—

2 If the LORD had not been on our side
   when men attacked us,

3 then they would have swallowed us alive
   in their burning anger against us.

4 Then the waters would have engulfed us;
   the torrent would have swept over us;

5 the raging waters would have swept over us.

6 Praise the LORD,
   who has not let us be ripped apart by their teeth.

7 We have escaped like a bird from the hunter's net;
   the net is torn, and we have escaped.

8 Our help is in the name of the LORD,
   the Maker of heaven and earth.

PSALM 124:1-8 (The Message)

1 A pilgrim song of David. If God hadn't been for us —all together now, Israel, sing out!—

2 If God hadn't been for us when everyone went against us,

3 We would have been swallowed alive by their violent anger,

4 Swept away by the flood of rage, drowned in the torrent;

5 We would have lost our lives in the wild, raging water.

6 Oh, blessed be God! He didn't go off and leave us. He didn't abandon us defenseless, helpless as a rabbit in a pack of snarling dogs.

7 We've flown free from their fangs, free of their traps, free as a bird. Their grip is broken; we're free as a bird in flight.

8 God's strong name is our help, the same God who made heaven and earth.

I love the version from The Message. It helps you hear the psalm more readily as a song, doesn't it? Glance back at the first verse. Can't you hear the worship leader beginning the song and then coaxing the congregation to sing it like they mean it? *Louder, Israel! Every voice! All together now!* The image makes me smile.

Tom Mosley, the music and worship pastor at my home church, is one of my favorite people in the world. He has a wonderfully warm way of not letting our congregation get away with unenthusiastic, insincere worship. I can picture him saying something like, "I'm going to give you a second chance to sing that to God with all the affection and gratitude your heart can muster." That's a little of what the inspired writer of Psalm 124 was saying. I can almost hear him chide, "If God hasn't been good to you, don't bother. If He's never rescued you, save your breath. But if He has, and you know He has, lift your voices and give Him the praise due His name!"

I am so glad we have two days to consider this psalm because we're going to need ample time to relate and meditate. In his book *A Long Obedience in the Same Direction*, Eugene Peterson calls Psalm 124 "a song of hazard—and of help."[8] His description provided me with two perspectives to guide our two-day study on this wonderful song. Today we will focus on the hazards described in Psalm 124 and tomorrow we'll cast our gaze on the help. Take a look back at the HCSB translation of Psalm 124. The psalmist employed several metaphors or images to help us vividly picture the kind of peril that surrounds us.

PRINCIPAL QUESTION

List the metaphors in the left column. When you've finished your list, look up the Scriptures in the right-hand column and draw a line matching each metaphor to the one it reflects in Psalm 124.

Psalm 124 Metaphors	Similar Metaphors:
_____	
_____	Psalm 18:16-17
_____	Psalm 55:6-8
_____	Psalm 57:4

In Psalm 124 the psalmist described the vicious attacks of men like gaping jaws that seek to swallow us whole, like raging waters seeking to drown us, like teeth that try to rip us to shreds, and like fowlers' snares trying to capture us.

When was the last time you felt like someone or something was going to eat you alive? Describe the situation without using any names.

_____

When was the last time you felt like a situation was honestly going to drown you?

_____

"The engulfing waters

threatened me, the

deep surrounded me;

seaweed was wrapped

around my head."

Jonah 2:5, NIV

Jonah experienced this kind of torrent in the most literal sense. Your feet may never have touched salt water, yet surely somewhere along the way you've felt so tossed by angry waves that you could almost feel the seaweed wrapped around your head. Even now you may have to push it up out of your eyes to read your lesson. You caught the reference to human attack in Psalm 124:2. Our battle is not with flesh and blood but with powers of darkness (Eph. 6:10-12), but Satan successfully enlists human help in his scheme against us.

Our toughest challenges most often involve people rather than circumstances. People are much more difficult to get over than inanimate situations. Even if we haven't experienced many people's vicious attacks, we've encountered Satan's, whether or not we've realized it. We must let God open our eyes wide to the reality that we have a powerful enemy who—let me say this clearly—absolutely hates us.

Let's recapture what it feels like to be hated. Think back on your history with people for a moment because attack is much easier to identify in human terms.

Have you ever felt like another person despised you? ◯ yes ◯ no
If so, describe some of your feelings when you first realized it.

I've had the experience a few times, particularly in ministry. My feelings invariably get hurt and my first inclination is to ask, "Why? What have I done?" I am a dyed-in-the-wool people person. Sanguine to the bone, only on rare occasion do I fight a strong feeling of dislike for someone. I can only think of a couple of times that I've felt as if I honestly could not stand someone. So I always wonder—however naively—why he or she seems to detest me so. I also ask myself (and usually Keith, my sounding board) if I'm imagining it or if it's real. Let's settle something right here:

We who belong to Christ are not imagining that we have an enemy who hates us. *We do.* We also don't have to wonder why. Satan hates us because God loves us. He also hates us because we remind him of the position he lost. He was an anointed cherub. We are anointed children. He lost his place in heaven. Through Christ, we gained a place in heaven. Perhaps above all, Satan hatefully attacks us because he can't touch God. The closest he can come to hurting God is to hurt one of His children. Zechariah 2:8 says whoever touches one of God's children touches the apple of His eye. God will overlook an attack against you about as readily as He would overlook someone repeatedly poking Him in the eye.

When you feel attacked, how convinced are you that God is taking it personally and that you can trust Him to handle it as you seek and submit to Him?

1	2	3	4	5	6	7	8	9	10
Completely Unconvinced									*Completely Convinced*

As we grow increasingly convinced of the veracity of God's Word and His unwavering faithfulness, our times of turmoil will be considerably more bearable as He empowers us to confidently circle that "10." Let's make that confidence a goal.

Eugene Peterson says, "Among the Songs of Ascents, sung by the people of God on the way of faith, this is one that better than any other describes the hazardous work of all discipleship."[9] You and I have no idea the very real drama that surrounds us. The scenarios that we pay to see at the movies will ultimately pale in comparison to what Christian pilgrims have endured on our journeys to Mount Zion.

A vicious battle is being fought over your life—and right over your seaweed-wrapped head. You are not imagining that something's going on, and yes, it's more than meets the eye. From heaven's vantage point, your story is exceedingly more exciting than you can conceive—replete with dangers, near misses, and great escapes. As many bruises, scars, and successful hits as the enemy may have given us, as we study this psalm, I want you to celebrate that Satan didn't get all he wanted. That you're sitting here doing this Bible study is one of many proofs. The Devil had no such intention. He meant to destroy you.

Describe one time you were most aware of Satan's harmful intent.

_____

As much as your enemy may have stolen from you, think of something you believe in retrospect he wanted that he didn't get.

_____

One distinguishing element of Psalm 124 is its invitation to the reader to consider some what-if scenarios. It is "a narrative about what might have occurred without YHWH's aid."[10] "Throughout the psalm the praise is for deliverance from an *unrealized* condition that *might have been*"[11] (my emphasis). The following is a close rendering of the Hebrew in Psalm 124:2. "It was YHWH, but if it had not been …"[12]

I want to spend the rest of our lesson thinking about what might have been had God not rescued you. The purpose will be to jump on the page of Psalm 124, relate completely, and praise God with that same kind of fervor. Like me, you may feel that Satan got an ample leash and multiple punches. But Psalm 124 suggests that much worse would happened without God on our side. I'll go first; then it's your turn.

Before God interrupted my vocational path and told me I'd work for Him, I was majoring in pre-law, hotly pursuing the courtroom with my sights set on the politics. Had I remained unhealed from my past childhood abuse, I'm convinced I would have tried to prosecute my perpetrator over and over vicariously through similar situations. I would have taken my own lack of emotional health out on my profession. I was destined to be a crusader; and just like historical crusaders, I would have sinned grievously and called it righteous indignation. I don't believe that the thought of a defendant's innocence ever would have occurred to me in an accusation of abuse.

On a personal level, I believe I would have divorced several times as a means of self-fulfilling the prophecy that all men are rats. (Thank You, God, for saving me from such a sick assessment.) I most certainly would have been immoral, and yet because I had a heart for God, I would have nearly cried my eyes out about it later. Furthermore, I would have done every bit of this as the Christian I'd been since childhood. I'm not describing what my future would have been apart from salvation. I'm describing what my future would have been without the rip-roaring radical deliverance of Jesus Christ and His complete overthrow of every false Christ in my life.

PERSONAL QUESTION

What about you? What might have happened with your life "if the LORD had not been on [your] side"?

_____

_____

Now we can come alongside the writer of Psalm 124. Is God's interruption in the scenario you just described cause for praise? Conclude doing exactly that.

Day Five
Praise the Lord

TODAY'S TREASURE
"Praise the Lord, who has not let us be ripped apart by their teeth."
Psalm 124:6, HCSB

I've thought so much about our previous lesson. Imagining what our lives might have been like "if the LORD had not been on our side" is chilling, isn't it? Perhaps some of us still don't see ourselves falling into a pit of sin without God's radical deliverance, but outcomes of bitterness, coldness, and mean-spiritedness can be just as destructive as ethical and moral sins. In some ways they're more insidious because they're less recognizable. Think how despairing or self-destructive we would have become had God not rescued us.

I often reflect on how God delivered me from myself as much as from Satan. I would have ended up being my own worst enemy. For many years Satan got tremendous cooperation from me, but I finally came to a place where I vowed *no more*.

Has Satan effectively tempted you to oppose your own best interests? O yes O no
*If so, did you get fed up with being your own worst (earthly) enemy and decide to
let God bring you some healing?* O yes O no *What was the turning point?*

If you've not come to that turning point, don't feel condemned. Each of us holds an
invitation to take the next step with God. This journey may be to step out of self-
destruction and constant defeat and step up to more consistent victory.

*In our introductory session we talked about three historical associations with
the Psalms of Ascent. Check the three from the choices below. Try to complete
this exercise from memory, but check your notes from the introductory session
if the answers don't come easily. The Psalms of Ascent were ...*
O *associated with the 15 steps of the temple*
O *a compilation of David's songs when King Saul pursued him*
O *songs sung at the last supper*
O *songs sung on the pilgrimage to the Three Great Feasts*
O *songs sung by exiles returning to Jerusalem from captivity*

The third association we made in our introductory session was vital. The Psalms of
Ascent are strongly associated with the exiles returning from captivity. If you checked
the first, fourth, and fifth associations in the previous exercise, you were correct.

If you have been in the clutches of defeat, you have not come to this study through
a side door. God threw open the front door for you. You belong in this study, and if you
will let Him, God will usher you to a whole new level of freedom. Persevere in the study.
Attend each session. Do your homework. Fully engage and God will astound you. Let
Him have His healing way over the next four weeks and watch what He will do.

Now let's set both feet on the fifth step. We spent our first day on the hazards a
child of God faces and where we'd be had God not intervened. Today we center on
the specific kind of help emphasized in Psalm 124. We've already talked about God's
help in a couple of psalms, but we've only scratched the surface. God's help is all
encompassing; it comes in so many forms and scriptural assurances that we could
study nothing else for the remainder of our study and never run out of material. You
will discover that many psalms centering on God's help emphasize a different element
of divine aid. The kind of help Psalm 124 describes is very distinct. We read it yesterday, but I've purposely waited until today to camp on it.

Complete the following sentences drawn from verse 2.

HCSB: *"If the LORD had not been _____ ..."*

The Message: *"If GOD hadn't been _____ when everyone went against us."*

Imagine standing on a battlefield all alone facing an angry army of 1,000 men, each breathing torturous threats. Suddenly you feel the earth pound beneath your feet like the hoofbeats of 10,000 horsemen. Your heart nearly melts with fear as you prepare yourself for the ever-mounting foe. Then you realize it wasn't 10,000 horsemen after all. It was one. Your gaze lifts higher and higher as you try to focus on His face with the sun in your eyes. He looks 100 feet tall atop His stallion, and His very presence emanates authority. He is stunningly beautiful. Staggeringly powerful. His horse gallops onto the battlefield, kicking up the earth. The rider firmly pulls the reins and brings His horse to a halt right beside you. The horseman then looks down at you and says, "Proceed into battle, mighty warrior. I am on your side."

What does Joshua 23:10 say? _____

_____

When we call on His name, God promises believers power and victory in the terrifying battles of the spiritual realm. He promised we'd be <u>more than</u> conquerors.

When we call upon His name, God promises New Testament believers that same kind of power and victory in the far more terrifying battles of the spiritual realm. He didn't just promise we'd be conquerors. He promised we'd be *more than* conquerors. Christ will never take us into a battle we cannot win. We would have to choose defeat against our new nature. Why aren't we living with that kind of confidence? If I were a betting woman (something my grandmother always used to say), I'd wager a small fortune on the validity of this statement:

> Regardless of how long we've been Christians and how deeply we've studied God's Word, most of us don't really believe down in the marrow of our bones that God is entirely, wholeheartedly, and unwaveringly on our side.

We live most of our lives unconvinced that God is really *for us*. We have little trouble picturing ourselves on God's side, but for the life of us we can't picture God stooping down enough to be on ours. Even though we'll say things and sing things to the contrary, we live as if we believe down in the hidden places of our hearts and minds that God at best tolerates us. And lucky we are at that!

We may rarely admit it, but our actions, anxieties, fears, and insecurities suggest something else. Perhaps some of us don't so much feel as if God is *against* us as we just don't necessarily feel as if He's *for* us. We conclude that the only person God is truly for is Himself and rightly so, we reason.

Somewhere deep inside I think we're secretly convinced that God created man with very high hopes only to have them dashed. Forget divine foreknowledge and a Lamb slain before the foundation of the world. We proved a terrible disappointment to God, but because He is faithful to His covenant, He's obligated to see the plan to completion. Therefore, He tolerates us because He's stuck with us.

Be completely honest. Have you ever felt the way I just described? Think about how you often feel in the hidden recesses of your heart and what your actions, faith practices, and accepted limitations suggest.

On the scale below, estimate the position you tend to picture God taking with you.

God is against me   *God tolerates me*   *God is for me*

Meditate over your history with God for a moment. Regardless of where you marked the continuum, name a couple of things that helped shape that conclusion:

_____

_____

If you marked that you are most often convinced (actions bearing witness) that "God is for [you]" on the continuum, you've already answered this question.

Despite how we feel much of the time, can the rest of us think of a few times when we'd have to admit that God seemed to be on our side? Describe one of those times.

_____

_____

I'm hammering the point because I'd like to suggest that in our humanity we tend to determine whether God is *against* us, *for* us, or *tolerating* us based on how He appears to act in our circumstances. In other words, our litmus test for whether we think God is really for us is circumstantial evidence. If I don't get the promotion, God was for the other guy. If the relationship doesn't work out, God didn't root for me. If the cancer treatment doesn't take, I'm not a high priority to Him.

Give another similar assumption: _____

Don't for a moment think I'm minimizing the confusion any of these examples can cause as we try to picture God "on our side." John 13:7 continues to come to my mind with great relevance to our subject matter today.

Please write John 13:7 in the space below:

_____

_____

I well remember making decisions for my children they considered to be uncaring or even mean-spirited at the moment. I even used the words from time to time, "I am *for* you, child. For heaven's sake, I'm your mother! Why wouldn't I want what's best for you?" I remember times when one of them would claim with great drama, "You hate me!" She was too young and immature to understand that my decision was *for* her.

What invariably hurt most was if one of the children charged me with making the decision selfishly because I didn't want to go to the extra trouble a yes answer would necessitate. Sometimes I couldn't convince them otherwise, so I'd have to temporarily live with them thinking poorly of me and questioning my motives. I wanted to be popular with my children. I didn't want to make decisions that could be misunderstood. Still, the future ramifications were worth the present misunderstanding.

On a much greater scale, God can take a similar position. He knows when something glorious in the future necessitates something difficult in the present. Because He knows the glory will be worth it, God will risk being misunderstood. Yes, God wants us to have joyful, satisfying lives, but He also wants us to have crowns to cast. Rewards to receive. Character to develop. Compassion to give. Testimonies to tell. In the midst of those painful processes, God makes bold promises.

PERSONAL QUESTION

Read Romans 8:28-39 and let God tell you what He'll do for you. Make this exercise personal by putting your name in the top blank and filling in the remainder with various promises God makes you in the portion from Romans. Turn each into an "I will" statement from God to you. I'll fill in the first one so you'll get the idea.

My child, _____

I will *make sure all things work together for your good.* _____

I will _____ .

I will _____ .

I will _____ .

I will _____ .

I will _____ .

Love, God

Those are promises, Dear One. Promises God made straight to you. He is not against you. He does not just tolerate you. He doesn't stick around because He feels obligated to you. God is on your side because He chooses to be.

A few days ago I received word of a group in Cape Town, South Africa, going through the Bible study *Breaking Free*. The woman leading the study shared that a prostitute wandered in off the street while the class was underway. The troubled woman was simply looking for a place to sit and rest her weary frame. As our wonderful God would have it, she ended up listening to the entire class, approached the leader, and said, "I can never go back to my old life."

When I heard the story, I wept. That, Beloved, is one reason I love Jesus so much. He is the ultimate Prince Charming to every woman, especially the one who forgot she was Cinderella. He looked with loving eyes on that lifeless woman, knowing all she'd ever said and done. He gazed beneath her sin into the brokenness that caused her to devalue herself so thoroughly. He'd given His whole life for her and wanted her to know that she was worth it to Him. Christ, the Spotless One and the Righteous King, saw beauty beneath her wounded, weathered exterior and sought to make her His own. As surely as Jesus met the Samaritan woman at the well in John 4, He drew a South African prostitute to the fountain of living Water and gave her a drink. Despite her self-destruction, Christ was for her. He was on her side when she was her own worst enemy. That's the way He is.

He's on your side.

Please conclude by writing Psalm 124 in your own words. Fill in the next step on your stair graphic with words best describing what you've learned from this psalm.

My Psalm 124

viewer guide

Our Eyes Look to the Lord

In our introduction we talked about the strong association between the Psalms of Ascent and the Three Great Feasts or Pilgrim Feasts. Today we will consider the first of those feasts; in sessions 3 and 4 we'll consider the next two. We will consider each of the feasts and the parallels they pose to us as New Testament sojourners on our way to the heavenly Jerusalem.

Part One

The Old Testament Emphasis on the Feast *(Read Lev. 23:4-11,14 and Deut. 16:1-4.)*

• The first of the Pilgrim Feasts was the Feast of _____

_____.

• This feast began at sundown at the conclusion of Passover and lasted for the

next _____ days.

• They ate unleavened bread on the first Passover because they were to eat in

_____, ready at any moment to _____.

Part Two

The New Testament Emphasis on the Feast

• See Luke 2:41 for the first mention of Jesus' own participation.

• See Matthew 16:5-9. Leaven became symbolic of _____. *The Feasts of the Lord* explains "In Hebrew, leaven is known as *chametz,* which literally means

'_____.' Leaven (usually yeast or baking powder) is used to

produce _____" *The Feasts of the Lord* goes on to say

that "ancient rabbis also believed that leaven represents the _____

_____ of the heart."[1] This fermentation implied a process of

_____.

- *International Standard Bible Encyclopedia* adds an interesting picture of the

  process: The "leaven" consisted, so far as the evidence goes, of a piece of

  fermented dough _____ _____ from a _____ _____…

  The lump of dough thus preserved was either dissolved in water in the knead

  ing trough before the flour was added, or was "_____" in the flour …

  and kneaded along _____ it. Compare 1 Corinthians 5:7-8.

Part Three

The Symbolism Fulfilled in Christ

- Read Matthew 26:17,26; then consider Acts 2:29-33.
- Recall Leviticus 23:4-11.

  According to *The Feasts of the Lord* …

  (1) Passover pictures the _____ of the Messiah.

  (2) The Feast of Unleavened Bread pictures the _____

      of the Messiah.

  (3) Firstfruits pictures the _____ of the Messiah.

      (See 1 Cor. 15:20-24.)

1. Adapted from Kevin Howard and Marvin Rosenthal, *The Feasts of the Lord* (Nashville: Thomas Nelson, 1997), 65-72.

Psalm 125

...song of ascents.

...t in the LORD are like
...on, shaken but endures
...erusalem,
...ll not
...people

Week Three
Great Things for Us

Principal Questions
1. What metaphor do Psalm 125:1 and Psalm 30:6-7 share?
2. How did God describe Himself in Zechariah 2:5?
3. According to Psalm 126:1-3, what kinds of things did the Israelites feel and experience?
4. How does Galatians 6:9 convey the element of time in the process of harvest?
5. How are the words of King David's beloved son in Ecclesiastes 1:2 thematically similar to Psalm 127:1-2?

Day One: He Surrounds His People
Day Two: A Love that Surrounds
Day Three: To Laugh Again
Day Four: Sowing the Seed
Day Five: Vain Labor

Day One
He Surrounds His People

TODAY'S TREASURE

"Jerusalem—the mountains surround her. And the LORD surrounds His people, both now and forever."
Psalm 125:2, HCSB

I love studying with you more than I can describe. I am blessed by anyone I can serve, but my life is completely wrapped up in serving Jesus through serving women. I get a huge kick out of us. I laughed my head off with my Bible study group in Houston last night. They are just about as animated as their teacher. They cry easily and laugh copiously. They are my home girls, and I'm nuts about them. But I'm also nuts about the rest of you. I spent last weekend with a civic center full of women gathered in Charleston, West Virginia. They were gloriously rowdy from the very beginning, so I knew we were going to have a good time with Jesus. They had come for Him, and nothing on earth was going to stop them from having Him. Not even an obnoxious Bible teacher who will apparently stop at nothing to make a point.

I have flashbacks of some women from Canada handing me a small Canadian flag that I promptly stuck in my up-do and wore for a good while. I'm humiliated in hindsight by some of the ridiculous things I"ve done with a group that at the time seemed perfectly appropriate. Maybe you and I individually are not the problem. Maybe you bring out the weirdness in me just like the women in West Virginia whose T-shirts pictured me from the early 1980s. In case you were asleep or not yet born then, my hair was the size of a beach ball and just about as many colors. The women got the picture out of the family book I wrote called *Feathers from My Nest*. With great mirth I included the Easter snapshot captioned: "The five of us: Keith, Beth, Amanda, Melissa, and Beth's Hair." My mane had a persona all its own. The women from West Virginia had captions on the back of their shirts, "Big Hair for Jesus." Do you see what I mean? How am I supposed to act normal when I serve people who are that loony?

Whether opposites or neuroses attract, I guess we belong together on this pilgrimage. I could have no greater delight than walking with you on this leg of the journey to our Mount Zion where we'll finally see our Savior's face. Step by step He will reveal the path of life to us, and we will experience inexpressible joy in His presence (see Ps. 16:11). Every obstacle we face and every battle we fight on the way will be worth it.

We get to put one foot on the sixth step of our pilgrimage of ascent today. Psalm 125 will be our text both today and tomorrow. I hope you've had a chance to take your place on your face today. If not, perhaps you could do so before the day is over. Like Joshua, you and I want to hear what our Master has to say to us (see Josh. 5:14b). I'm not sure a pair of ears is ever better exposed than when the face connecting them is flat on the floor. Let's get started with Psalm 125. *Say it, work it;* then at the conclusion of our next lesson, *pray it.*

PSALM 125 *(HCSB)*

Israel's Stability

A song of ascents.

1 Those who trust in the LORD are
   like Mount Zion.
   It cannot be shaken; it remains forever.
2 Jerusalem—the mountains surround her.
   And the LORD surrounds His people,
   both now and forever.
3 The scepter of the wicked will not remain
   over the land allotted to the righteous,
   so that the righteous will not apply their hands
   to injustice.
4 Do what is good, LORD, to the good,
   to those whose hearts are upright.
5 But as for those who turn aside to crooked ways,
   the LORD will banish them with the evildoers.
   Peace be with Israel.

PSALM 125 *(NCV)*

God Protects Those Who Trust Him

A song for going up to worship.

1 Those who trust the Lord are like Mount Zion,
   which sits unmoved forever.
2 As the mountains surround Jerusalem,
   the Lord surrounds his people
   now and forever.
3 The wicked will not rule
   over those who do right.
   If they did, the people who do right
   might use their power to do evil.
4 Lord, be good to those who are good,
   whose hearts are honest.
5 But, Lord, when you remove those who do evil,
   also remove those who stop following you.
Let there be peace in Israel.

Today you and I will steep ourselves entirely in the first verse and the picture it draws. How does verse 1 describe the people who trust in the Lord?

_____

The Hebrew word for "trust" in verse 1 is "batach," defined as being "confident, secure, sure."[1] Each of those three words carries its own distinct connotation, so let's fill in Psalm 125:1 with each one in the order offered by the definition.

"Those who [are _____] in the LORD are like Mount Zion. It cannot be shaken; it remains forever." How would you describe confidence in the Lord?

_____

"Those who [are _____] in the LORD are like Mount Zion. It cannot be shaken; it remains forever." How would you describe security in the Lord?

_____

"Those who [are _____] in the LORD are like Mount Zion. It cannot be shaken; it remains forever." How would you describe being sure about the Lord?

_____

The word between "confident" and "sure" encompasses all the rest. The Hebrew word for "trust" in Psalm 125:1 means finding every bit of our security in the Lord our God, unseen though He is. I love the sound of the word *secure*. I love the real, live feeling of it even more, I suppose, because I spent most of my life looking for it. Few things in the human experience breed misery more than insecurity.

PERSONAL QUESTION

Can you think of a few ways insecurity has caused you some misery? If so, please share them as honestly as you can.

_____

_____

Check each of these conditions that could be rooted in insecurity:

- O Jealousy
- O Low self-worth
- O Envy
- O Promiscuity
- O Manipulation
- O Unbelief

Add a few more that come to mind: _____

_____

Insecurity has remained one of my most consistent challenges, and because I'm convinced it's epidemic in our deceived culture, I hammer it in almost every Bible study. In my opinion, each of the painful conditions above is rooted in insecurity. Yesterday I received a sweet letter from a sister in Christ who was taking the *Daniel* Bible study. She concluded her gracious note of encouragement with the words, "For the life of me, I cannot understand why you are insecure."

You would be surprised to know how many people who seem to have it all together are chronically insecure. Though insecurity can be rooted in all sorts of experiences, I have a feeling that many of us share the same one. When key people in your formative years were supposed to bring you security but brought insecurity instead, you inherit a tremor in your soul that is impossible to naturally still. Add to it all the times you let yourself down and fail to measure up like I did, and naturally speaking, you're a piece of earth in a constant quake.

I don't live in defeat over it much of the time, but Satan knows that insecurity is an effective temptation for me. I don't think victory over insecurity will ever come to me automatically. God and I dialogue about it consistently, and He alone has proved strong enough to quell my insecurity.

Insecurity is a serious problem, but self-security can be an even bigger problem—even self-security drawn from our position as a child of God. Consider Psalm 125:1 and a contrasting image drawn by David in Psalm 30:6-7. "When I was secure, I said, 'I will never be shaken.' LORD, when You showed Your favor, You made me stand like a strong mountain; when You hid Your face, I was terrified" (HCSB).

"Those who trust in the LORD are like Mount Zion. It cannot be shaken; it remains forever."
Psalm 125:1, HCSB

What metaphor do Psalm 125:1 and Psalm 30:6-7 share?

Both passages speak of conditions that make a person like a mountain, unshakable and strong. Psalm 30:6-7, however, speaks of a mountain-like security in past tense. "When I *was* secure" (emphasis mine). I wonder if the psalmist grew a little overconfident. I'm not talking about overconfidence in God because Scripture renders such a condition impossible. I wonder if David may have grown a little overconfident in God's manifest favor.

Glance back at Psalm 30:6-7 and write the psalmist David's first sentence, emphasizing each "I" by making the letter larger than the others.

The New King James Version draws a clearer picture of David's past-tense security: "Now in my prosperity I said, 'I shall never be moved.' LORD, by Your favor You have made my mountain stand strong; You hid Your face, *and* I was troubled."

What wording does this version use instead of "when I felt secure"?

Consider this carefully: David was the first to ascribe his prosperity to the Lord, but somewhere along the way he mistakenly placed his security in the blessing of God rather than God Himself. We often know enough not to ascribe our security to carnal, worldly things. Our greater and slyer temptation is to place our security in the blessings we readily credit to the Lord.

Even if our security is in something God has given us—our gifts, talents, loved ones, church family, consistent victory, passion for His Word—our seemingly secure mountain ultimately will fall into the sea. We can grow secure in the favor God has shown us, but God's favor and His person are not synonymous. If our trust is in manifestations of God's favor rather than God Himself, we will crumble like dry clay when He calls us to walk a distance of our journeys entirely by faith and not by sight.

To build on our previous psalm of ascent, God is with us and for us even when His face and His favor seem hidden. Mountain-like security only comes from trusting God, not what He's done for us or given us, however glorious and eternal those things may be.

The difference between trusting God and trusting what God has done is a fine line we easily can trip over, falling headlong into a pit just as David feared. Thankfully, he described what to do in the subsequent verses of Psalm 30. We can do likewise when we realize we have unknowingly let our security slip from God Himself to His manifest favor. Let these words resonate in your sweet soul today.

"I cried out to You, O LORD; And to the Lord I made supplication: 'What profit *is there* in my blood, When I go down to the pit? Will the dust praise You? Will it declare Your truth? Hear, O LORD, and have mercy on me; LORD, be my helper!' You have turned for me my mourning into dancing; You have put off my sackcloth and clothed me with gladness, To the end that *my* glory may sing praise to You and not be silent. O LORD my God, I will give thanks to You forever" (Ps. 30:8-12, NKJV).

Day Two

A Love That Surrounds

One of my deepest desires is for God to take each of us to the next level of worship. He wants to actively develop the psalmist in each of us. I'm writing you today from our little cabin. My daughter, Amanda, and my darling grandson, Jackson, are here with Keith and me. To our unending delight, Jackson is forming an attachment to his grandparents, and we're shamelessly at his beck and call. Keith and Beanie have gone grouse hunting, and I'm on the porch in the cool autumn breeze, gazing at the distant Grand Teton Mountains through flickering yellow aspen leaves. Jackson is on the den floor kicking his legs and cooing to a baby praise DVD. Children's voices singing the words "I was born to worship" are flowing through the speakers, causing my eyes to burn with tears. Yes, Jackson, you were. So was I. And so, Dear One, were you.

Jackson's parents and grandparents want more than anything for him to have a psalmist's heart to worship Jesus. In addition to the training from birth from his God-praising parents, he's had some proactive praise dancing lessons with yours truly. I want him to know that nothing brings the heart, soul, and mind greater joy and satisfaction than praising the one true God. I never want Jackson to associate worship with boredom or to incessantly check his watch to see when the service will be over.

No, I don't think worship has to always be boisterous and loud for us to stay engaged, but I also don't think it has to be so austere that we'd rather watch the bowling finals. Jackson is in that wonderful stage when babies babble all sorts of syllables. Amanda and I love to playfully interpret. She just interrupted my soapbox by saying, "If I didn't know better, I'd tell you Jackson just said *hallelujah.*" Well, of course he did! He's his grandmother's grandson! Actually, of course, he didn't. He's just eight months old. But some day he will, and I intend to be there. Dancing.

TODAY'S TREASURE

"As the mountains surround Jerusalem, the LORD surrounds his people now and forever."
Psalm 125:2, NCV

OK, Dear Worshiper, let's return to Psalm 125. Turn to our previous lesson and read either version. Check here when you've finished. _____

On day 1 we focused on the metaphor of an unshakable mountain as depicted in Psalm 125:1. Today we'll do likewise regarding the imagery drawn by the psalmist's words in verse 2.

How did the psalmist describe God's position regarding His people (v. 2)?

_____

What do these verses say about God's help and sustaining presence?

Psalm 34:7 _____

Psalm 139:5 _____

Now read the wonderful prophetic vision God gave the prophet Zechariah regarding Jerusalem in Zechariah 2:3-5. How did God describe Himself in verse 5?

_____

What an amazing picture! Reflect on it for a moment. Picture yourself in the middle of it. God has you surrounded. His presence looms over you from every direction. "As the mountains surround Jerusalem, the Lord surrounds his people now and forever" (Ps. 125:2, NCV). Nothing can close in on you without closing in on Him first. God alone can be both the watchman and the wall. He has you surrounded even when you don't want Him anywhere near you because of sin. Boy, have I been there. As much as I wanted God to move away from me in my humiliation, I was never more thankful for His surrounding presence than when I'd hide my face in a pillow and sob His name and sense Him say, "I'm right here. I never moved."

If you are in Christ, you can't get rid of Him. You can't outrun or hide from Him. At no time is He inattentive. At no time have you caught Him off guard. Picture yourself on that school playground again. You're blindfolded, playing a game with giggling friends encircling you. No matter how many times you turn round and round and dizzily stop to randomly point to the person who is "it," "it" will be God every time.

You may be a visual learner like I am, so perhaps you too relish colorful metaphors like craggy mountains surrounding vulnerable people. I like something even better than pretty pictures, however. I like practical truths. If God has us surrounded like a chain of mighty mountains, then why have we suffered so much harm?

You don't have to wince or glance around to see if anyone caught you reading the question. The psalms offer a divine invitation for us to ask hard questions and grapple with difficult and sometimes eerily absent answers.

Keep in mind that God gave each of us a brain for spiritual reasons as well as intellectual reasons. He doesn't mean for us to unscrew our heads and take them off when we study the Bible. If God says He has us surrounded, yet we feel we've been viciously attacked, He doesn't mind our bringing Him our confusion. Do we reconcile the matter by supposing that God has us surrounded until some great evil breaks His grip? Beloved, if God is not more powerful than all the combined evil in the universe, we are a pitiful people indeed. The same psalm that told us "the angel of the LORD encamps around those who fear him, and he delivers them" (Ps. 34:7, NIV) offers us help balancing the issue.

Read Psalm 34:17-19 and record everything you learn about God's help.

_____

_____

God's great deliverance in itself presupposes a trouble from which the person was delivered. God's closeness to the brokenhearted presupposes a difficulty that broke the heart. The depth of God's aid to the crushed in spirit presupposes the occurrence of something crushing. Psalm 34:19 (NKJV) says, "Many are the afflictions of the righteous, But the LORD delivers him out of them all."

God never promised to remove us from human experience, but for those of us who call Jesus Savior, the only difficulty we'll ever experience will be right here. The New Testament echoes Psalm 34:19 in numerous places. One of them is Acts 14:22 where we're told of Paul and Barnabas "strengthening the hearts of the disciples by encouraging them to continue in the faith, and by telling them, 'It is necessary to pass through many troubles on our way into the kingdom of God' " (HCSB).

"On our way into the kingdom," God's absolute priority is relationship. Carefully read Psalm 116:1-7. What were the first words out of the psalmist's mouth?

_____

Why did he love the Lord so much (vv. 1-2)? _____

Describe the seriousness of the psalmist's circumstances (v. 3). _____

_____

Even after being allowed to endure overwhelming anguish, how did the psalmist

describe God (vv. 5-6)? _____

_____

Review verse 7 and compare it with a specific petition in Psalm 125:4, our present Psalm of Ascent. What is the theme of both verses?

_____

OK, let's confront the bottom line. How can we say God has been good to us when He has allowed us to encounter trouble and sorrow? Share your honest thoughts.

_____

_____

_____

PERSONAL QUESTION

God's delivering us *from* every ounce of trial will never develop the relationship that occurs when God shows Himself faithful right in the midst of difficulty, delivering us *through* it. That's where we come to know Him, to love Him, to appreciate Him. Call me immature, but as I drive the freeways of Houston, I'm not nearly as prone to give God praise when I have no idea what near-miss I just experienced. Let something deadly almost happen and I am in full-throttle dialogue with my ever-present God.

What about when something deadly happens such as when we lost loved ones who loved God? Where was God's surrounding presence then? That's where the ultimate trust enters in. If we believe God's words are true, when tragedy strikes we've got to believe God has us so tightly interwoven in His care that we are instantaneously swept to heaven. God never more closely surrounds us than when He lifts us to His breast and carries us home. If evil was involved, we must trust God to avenge the wrong just as the writer of Psalm 125 believed He would do (vv. 3,5). No matter how kind we want to be, our souls have deep need to know that God will deal with the wicked. Thankfully, Scripture makes that promise more than a few times.

A dyed-in-the-wool traveler, I love learning about world cultures. Keith and I have been to a number of places in Africa where we were invited to glimpse lifestyles rich in traditions vastly different from ours. The Maasai people of Kenya left me with an image of God's encircling protection that I'll never forget. Trying their hardest to resist modern influences, the Maasai move from place to place along the vast countryside, depending on their livestock's needs. We were welcomed into several villages surrounded by hedges of thorn bushes erected to deter predators. Keith couldn't get over the spiritual significance for Christians, remarking to me that God keeps His people safe from the prowling lion by encircling us with a crown of thorns. I've often thought about his metaphor and prayed that very image for my loved ones.

In my human nature, I am a worrier, particularly concerning the lives of my loved ones. One hazard of this ministry is that I'm privy to so many shocking stories and tragedies that I don't have the luxury of naiveté. If I don't deliberately fight a spirit

God never more closely surrounds us than when He lifts us to His breast and carries us home.

of fear, it can overtake me with staggering force. How about you? Who are you most prone to worry about? If they are Christians, write their names in the crown of thorns above, praying your own version of Psalm 125 as you do so. Entrust each loved one to God's care. Picture this metaphor daily until your anxieties diminish, even if the process takes months. If the people who concern you most are not Christians, write their names by faith within the circle, draw a cross over them, and ask God to surround them so tightly they surrender. This exercise may seem elementary, but visuals like this help me tremendously. I pray you are helped as well, Dear One.

Like the mountains surrounding Jerusalem, God is ever surrounding us. He sees and sifts every life experience that could touch His child. Nothing can break His grip.

Remember to write your own version of Psalm 125 and fill in your stair graphic with the most profound truth God revealed to you personally through this psalm. You are wonderful, Beloved. Christ greatly esteems your diligence.

My Psalm 125

Day Three
To Laugh Again

I dearly love Psalm 126. I memorized it before I had the joy of experiencing what it describes. In my late twenties God began putting me through an intense course of Scripture memorization that I realized later was like a spiritual bone marrow transplant (see Heb. 4:12). I had no idea the kind of captivity that still held me. I'd never heard the word *stronghold* as a scriptural concept or potential reality in the life of a believer. At that time, a stronghold was something I looked for in my hair spray. In retrospect, I believe God wanted me well equipped with Scripture when He allowed the enemy the longest leash he's ever had in my life.

In a similar way Christ allowed Satan greater access to Peter in Luke 22:31-32, I believe God permitted the enemy to sift me like wheat in my early thirties. The experience is part of my testimony, and I continue to share it because I don't want others caught off guard by the enemy's schemes. My faithful Father allowed this excruciating process, first of all, because I had something that needed sifting. God is practical. He doesn't allow people to be sifted who have nothing they need radically extracted from their lives.

Second, Jesus knew something I didn't. He knew that even after the severest beating of my life and by far the deepest brokenness, He'd forgive me, heal me, crucify that self-destructive part of me, and stand me back on my feet through the measureless power of His Spirit. Instead of being finished for life, which I could have easily assumed, Christ sent me forth in the echo of Luke 22:32 to strengthen my sisters. Strangely, it was not the end of ministry. It was the beginning. An entire Bible study ministry followed those dreadfully dark days when despair overtook me.

Christ is both Alpha and Omega. When our lives are immersed in Him, every ending, everything we believe to be the death of us is instead a hand-engraved invitation to a new beginning. God is so much better than He has to be. The kinds of things God chooses to do in our lives that are "immeasurably more than we ask or imagine" (Eph. 3:20, NIV) are not out of obligation. They gush from unbridled affection.

A few nights ago I returned from a conference in Salt Lake City where God poured out a lavish anointing of His Spirit, wooed 55 women to receive His Son as their Savior, and altered a few thousand other lives, including mine. I sat in the bed that night in my pajamas and wept with gratitude, asking Him for at least the one thousandth time why He has allowed me to serve Him and to serve women like you. The only answer I've ever been able to discern in response is something like this: "Because I want to. That's why."

TODAY'S TREASURE

"Our mouths were filled with laughter then, and our tongues with shouts of joy. Then they said among the nations, 'The LORD has done great things for them.' "
Psalm 126:2, HCSB

God doesn't do these divine works because He *has* to. He does them because He *wants* to. To move to the next level with God, we have to feel that He wants us there, that we're invited. Let's keep nailing down a point. God doesn't just tolerate us or remain with us out of obligation. We are His treasure and the objects of His holy passion. Get that through your darling little thick skull today.

Dive into Psalm 126. *Say it, work it;* then at the end of day 4, we'll *pray it.*

PSALM 126 *(HCSB)*

Zion's Restoration
A song of ascents.
1 When the LORD restored the fortunes of Zion,
    we were like those who dream.
2 Our mouths were filled with laughter then,
    and our tongues with shouts of joy.
    Then they said among the nations,
    "The LORD has done great things for them."
3 The LORD had done great things for us;
    we were joyful.
4 Restore our fortunes, LORD,
    like watercourses in the Negev.
5 Those who sow in tears
    will reap with shouts of joy.
6 Though one goes along weeping,
    carrying the bag of seed,
    he will surely come back with shouts of joy,
    carrying his sheaves.

PSALM 126 *(The Message)*

1 A pilgrim song
    It seemed like a dream, too good to be true,
    when GOD returned Zion's exiles.
2 We laughed, we sang, we couldn't believe our
    good fortune. We were the talk of the nations—
    "GOD was wonderful to them!"
3 GOD was wonderful to us; we are one happy
    people.
4 And now, GOD, do it again— bring rains to
    our drought-stricken lives
5 So those who planted their crops in despair
    will shout hurrahs at the harvest,
6 So those who went off with heavy hearts will
    come home laughing, with armloads of blessing.

Psalm 126 falls conveniently into perfect halves. **The Message** *makes the transition clearest. Write the verse that you think introduces the second half:*

_____

_____

The first three verses testify to something wonderful, dramatic, and gracious God did in the past. The second three verses petition God to do something like it again. James Limburg words the time frame beautifully in his commentary on the psalms. "Psalm 126 comes from a people who are living between the times, between a good time remembered and another good time hoped for."[2]

Draw a simple time line below depicting and labeling what Limburg described.

At the left you may have written something like, "A good time remembered." Toward the right you might have said, "Another good time hoped for." Hopefully, in between you captured the idea of "living between the times." Are you there now? Me too! Push the hold button, and let's first reflect on "another good time remembered." Meditate on something wonderful and tremendously freeing God did for you.

If you stay in the spirit of Psalm 126, you won't have to wrack your brain to remember. It will be something God did for you that you couldn't easily forget. If you are new in your walk with God and have not yet experienced something like this, allow the next paragraphs to build your faith for what is yet to come if you keep trusting and obeying Him. On the other hand, those who have experienced a wonderfully dramatic work of God can revel in the memory of His grace and goodness.

PRINCIPAL QUESTION

Many scholars agree that Psalm 126 describes the Israelites when they were set free from Babylonian captivity and allowed to return to Jerusalem. Read the first three verses again carefully. What kinds of things did they feel and experience?

_____

_____

Have you ever experienced something almost too good to be true? The psalmist described a time when God did something so glorious and undeserved for the Israelites they felt they had to be dreaming. They couldn't keep from laughing. Their new reality seemed so absurdly opposite from where they'd been that God alone could have done it. Surely after they were released from Babylon they looked back thinking their captors would change their minds as the Egyptians had. How many times do you think they glanced over their shoulders, saw no enemy gaining on them, and said, "I can't believe this! We've got to be dreaming!"

How did Peter's experience in Acts 12:3-11 parallel the exiles in Psalm 126:1-3?

_____

Two experiences come most quickly to my mind as I reflect on such wonderful times. One was when the first Bible study, *A Woman's Heart, God's Dwelling Place,* hit the bookstore shelves. Keith had called the store to find out the exact day the study would be stocked; then he surprised me and took me there. We both stood in the bookstore aisle and wept. Neither of us said a word because we knew what the other was thinking. It was a miracle. Surely God had never used anyone more broken and tainted. The second memory that jumps into my mind is the evening of Keith's and my twenty-fifth anniversary when we said our vows again with a minister and with our daughters as our attendants. We are a miracle.

PERSONAL QUESTION

Now it's your turn. Describe a time when God did something that you could hardly believe and knew you didn't deserve.

Underneath the segment on the time line that says something like *a good time remembered,* write a phrase describing the event. Isn't having laughter restored to our souls after a time of sadness and drought just the best? I love to laugh, and I cherish knowing when it's a divine gift that has come like a huge bow on a package of restoration.

Now let's think about the remaining parts of the time line. Reflect back on Limburg's words. "Psalm 126 comes from a people who are living between the times, between a good time remembered and another good time hoped for."[3] Could the verses of Psalm 126 describe you? Have you seen wonderful works of God in the past but you could really use one now? You may be in a terrible situation right now.

Take heart that God sees you and is moved by your plight. He still performs wonders. Don't let anyone tell you otherwise. Profess your belief to Him daily that you will see the evidence of His gracious hand and, like the psalmist David, stay confident of this: "I will see the goodness of the LORD in the land of the living. Wait for the LORD; be strong and take heart and wait for the LORD" (Ps. 27:13-14, NIV).

Or you may be in my position. I am not in peril or a deep valley right this moment, but I have seen huge wonders of God in the past and I want to see them again! As Eugene Peterson writes, "And now, God, do it again!"[4] I want an "again" work of God in my life. Do you? Then let's allow Psalm 126 to be just the motivation we need to ask for it. God has not run out of wonders where we are concerned, Beloved. We have not seen the last great work of God in our lives. Perish the thought! We haven't used up our quota of God's mercies for the year. Let's ask, Dear One!

Go back to your time line again and under the portion representing "another good time hoped for," write the nature of the work you hope God will accomplish.

As you do, be absolutely confident that God will act and that He will be faithful even if the work ends up looking different than you described. Though God may know a better way, He welcomes us to make our hearts' desires known to Him.

Conclude by returning to your time line. Under the portion representing the time "in between," confess several of your fears about the future to the God who loves you. When you finish, write over the words you have written: "Jeremiah 29:11." Look up the Scripture and choose with every part of your being to believe it.

You and I will never move to the next level with God if we're scared half to death of what awaits us. On this mysterious pilgrimage we will find that when we do meet difficulties and sorrows, they were not meant to stop us but to form the character required for our great harvest in the coming season. Step into your future, Precious One. Something wonderful awaits you.

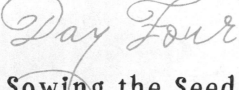

Sowing the Seed

Houston fights with fall every October. Tropical girl that she is, she arm wrestles autumn with such fierceness that every year we fear she'll win and summer will never leave us. As I write, it's that dreadful time again. The head-on collision in the atmosphere is shooting lightning across the sky and pounding our soggy ground with enough water to worry Noah. We live practically this entire season on a tornado watch.

Changes of seasons in our lives or moving on with God can come with the same ferocity. Sometimes we find ourselves on the next step, unsure how we got there. Other times we fight with everything we've got to get there. We must be willing to fight. The more Satan sees something crucial on that next step, the more he will fight you.

Why does God allow such warfare? Sometimes God uses the fight to strengthen muscles we'll need at that next level. If yesterday's wimp is going to become tomorrow's warrior, something has to happen *today*.

I'm filled with anticipation as we continue. Today we'll study the second half of Psalm 126.

Please turn back to day 3 and read either translation of the psalm, giving special attention to verses 4-6. Today we center on the statements in the last two verses. Does Psalm 126:5-6 sound more like a …

○ *hope*   ○ *proverb*   ○ *promise*   ○ *prayer*   ○ *lie*

TODAY'S TREASURE
"Those who sow in tears will reap with shouts of joy."
Psalm 126:5, HCSB

Complete the following according to the HCSB *to confirm your answer.*

"Those who sow in tears _____ *reap with shouts of joy" (v. 5).*

"Though one goes along weeping, carrying the bag of seed, he _____ _____ *come back with shouts of joy, carrying his sheaves" (v. 6).*

I don't know about you, Beloved, but those verses sound like outright unapologetic promises to me. But they are conditional promises.

Turn the following Scriptures around, listing the promise and the condition of each:

Promise: You will ...   Condition: If you ...

Psalm 126:5

_____   _____

Psalm 126:6

_____   _____

I want what these verses promise. I need to know I'll never endure a season of tears that can't turn into a harvest of joy. I'd be willing to meet almost any condition God would offer. You too?

Let's start taking the promises and conditions apart until we understand what they mean. Since the conditions involve sowing seed, we'll draw our parallel to the seed from Christ's own interpretation of the parable of the sower.

Please read Luke 8:11-15. What is the seed?

  ○ *The promises of God*   ○ *The Word of God*   ○ *The commands of God*

Why don't those depicted in verse 12 produce a crop? _____

_____

Why don't those depicted in verse 13 produce a crop? _____

_____

Why don't those depicted in verse 14 produce a crop? _____

_____

I need to know I'll never endure a season of tears that can't turn into a harvest of joy.

On the other hand, why do those depicted in verse 15 produce a crop?

About 15 months ago Keith and I went to war-torn Angola to do relief work and draw attention to tens of thousands of malnourished and famished people. We had been warned about the conditions we'd see, but I'm not sure anything could have prepared us for the reality. We saw townships with no electricity, no running water, no medical clinics or grocery stores. They had no means of contact with the outside world.

Many inhabitants had never been outside the village. Most of them wouldn't have a clue how to trek to a city to get food or help, and those who did were afraid of land mines left over from the war. Ours were the first white faces many of the children had ever seen, and since I rarely meet a child I can't soon win as a friend, I was humbled by some of their tears of terror. They thought they were seeing ghosts.

I've seen pictures of African children with golden hair since I was a little girl, but I had no idea that the lack of pigment indicates malnutrition. I will never forget the tiny legs that supported those bloated bellies as the children stood in lines as far as the eye could see to receive bowls of porridge we were dishing.

Keith and I were changed forever. We will do what we can for the poor as long as we live. I learned something in one of the rural villages that will mark my teaching and response to the Word of God. As we stood, trying to absorb the sights and smells of living death, our new friend, Isak Pretorius said, "One of the most frustrating things is that in villages where they receive seed, they often eat the seed rather than planting it and bringing forth the harvest." I couldn't get the statement out of my mind and suddenly had an answer to the questions I most often ask God: Why do some people see the results of the Word and others don't? Why do some study the Word of God yet remain in their captivity?

Some just eat the seed and never sow it for a harvest. You want examples? Why have many of us heard hundreds of messages on freedom, done every line of Bible studies like *Breaking Free,* wept over them, been blessed by them, and even memorized parts of them, yet remain in captivity? Because we ate the seed instead of sowing it. Why have many of us read books on forgiving people, known the teachings were true and right, cried over them, marked them up with our highlighters, yet remain in our bitterness? Because we ate the seed instead of sowing it. Why have we repeatedly heard how Christ has forgiven our sinful pasts and sobbed with gratitude over the grace of it, yet we remain in bondage to condemnation? Because we ate the seed instead of sowing it.

Sometimes we don't even realize the difference. We'll think we accepted the teaching because we were so moved by it. But you see, the seed of God's Word can fill our stomachs and give us immediate satisfaction and still not produce a harvest—that's when we eat it but don't sow it. Many times we apply biblical truth to our theologies without applying it to the actual practicalities of life. I know because I practiced this approach for years and could not understand why I was still in bondage.

I cannot say this loudly enough: God's Word is meant to be applied to our reality. We can "Amen!" the pastor as he preaches sacrificial love. We can walk to the car and comment on the great sermon he gave, drive home, and march in as mean and cold as the person who pulled out of the driveway. We decide surely God did not mean us to apply His truth to *our* reality because He knows how difficult this or that person is to love. What just happened? We ate the seed instead of sowing it.

By now I imagine you can think of your own example. What is it?

_____

Oh, Beloved, the last thing I want is to be harsh. I love you so. That's why I'm desperate for you to live in the reality of your God-promised victory. I'm concerned that many of us will eat the seed instead of sowing it. Then we charge God with unfaithfulness when we don't get the harvest He promised. God repeatedly says that a harvest is sown, not eaten as seed. We have to get down on our knees in the hardship of our circumstances and apply God's Word to the most difficult places, believing God will bring a harvest. Forgiving others, for instance, is a beautiful theology but a difficult reality. Those who apply it have a harvest for the rest of their lives. We were meant to eat from the sheaves, not from the seeds.

PRINCIPAL QUESTION

A harvest is never instant; it demands time. How does Galatians 6:9 convey the element of time in the process of harvest?

_____

If we don't see an immediate result from our acts of obedience, we often decide to dig up the seed and either eat it or cast it in the nearest ditch. Hebrews 6:12 was in my quiet time reading this morning. The second half of it applies beautifully to the wait implied by harvest. It tells us to "imitate those who through faith and patience inherit what has been promised" (NIV). Some of the inheritance God has promised each of us can only be received through faith and patience.

PERSONAL QUESTION

What part do you think faith and patience play in our wait as we obey God and look for the first sprouts of harvest?

Faith: _____

Patience: _____

82

Dear One, sowing the seed of God's Word in a terribly difficult situation is not easy! But God promises you—let me say that again—*absolutely promises you* that if you do, you will receive a harvest—and not just a harvest of any kind but a harvest of shout hallelujah joy! Are you game? Then get down on those knees and start digging in the ground of your reality and sow some seed. He who promised is faithful.

You are a great student of God's Word, Dear One. Whatever you do, don't just fill your tummy with this one. Sow it. Conclude your lesson today by praying your own Psalm 126; then be sure to fill in the appropriate step on your stair graphic.

My Psalm 126

Day Five

Vain Labor

We conclude the first half of our journey today. Let's celebrate our intentional God. I knew nothing about this compilation of pilgrim songs until He interrupted my thoughts and directed me to study them. Now the *Psalms of Ascent* have jumped to life and altered this pilgrim's path. Even if you were thoroughly familiar with them, I hope a fresh look has affected you too. As we seek God through His Word and desire to do His will, He fashions a tailor-made encounter. You have been pursued. Thank you for slowing down and letting Christ Jesus apprehend you with His love.

I hope Christ Jesus has spoken many truths to you throughout our first half of the journey, but think of one primary thing He's said to you so far. Keep listening for Him to confirm it; then respond with obedience and watch for the firstfruits of a harvest. As we wrap up our third week of study, we'll put one foot on the next step and set the other beside it on day 1 of week 4. Our text is Psalm 127. *Say it, work it;* then at the end of our next lesson, we'll *pray it.*

TODAY'S TREASURE

"Unless the LORD builds a house, its builders labor over it in vain; unless the LORD watches over a city, the watchman stays alert in vain."
Psalm 127:1, HCSB

PSALM 127 (HCSB)

A Solomonic song of ascents.

1 Unless the LORD builds a house,
   its builders labor over it in vain;
   unless the LORD watches over a city,
   the watchman stays alert in vain.
2 In vain you get up early and stay up late,
   eating food earned by hard work;
   certainly He gives sleep to the one He loves.
3 Sons are indeed a heritage from the LORD,
   children, a reward.
4 Like arrows in the hand of a warrior
   are the sons born in one's youth.
5 Happy is the man who has filled his quiver
   with them.
   Such men will never be put to shame
   when they speak with their enemies
   at the city gate.

PSALM 127 (NCV)

A song for going up to worship. Of Solomon.

1 If the Lord doesn't build the house, the builders are
   working for nothing.
   If the Lord doesn't guard the city, the guards are
   watching for nothing.
2 It is no use for you to get up early and stay up late,
   working for a living.
   The Lord gives sleep to those he loves.
3 Children are a gift from the Lord; babies are a reward.
4 Children who are born to a young man are like arrows
   in the hand of a warrior.
5 Happy is the man who has his bag full of arrows.
   They will not be defeated
   when they fight their enemies at the city gate.

Today we will concentrate on the first two verses of our present psalm of ascent, and on day 1 of our next unit we will focus on the remaining three.

Glance at the headings under both translations. To whom is this psalm attributed?

_____

Only two psalms, this one and Psalm 72, bear his name. Even divinely inspired authors often leave their fingerprints on their parchments. James Montgomery Boice points out that "there may be a cryptic reference to himself by Solomon in the words 'those he loves' (v. 2). In Hebrew the words are actually the name God gave Solomon according to 2 Samuel 12:25: Jedidiah, meaning 'Beloved of Jehovah.' "[5] The tone of the first two verses of Psalm 127 also rings with sounds of Solomon.

How are the words of King David's beloved son in Ecclesiastes 1:2 thematically similar to Psalm 127:1-2?

_____

PRINCIPAL QUESTION

The powerful message of Psalm 127:1-2 is that all labor spent on anything God Himself has not built is in vain. Founders of our great nation certainly understood the concept. Despite debates on whether Benjamin Franklin was a Christian or a Deist, his 1787 "Speech to the Convention for Forming a Constitution for the United States" in Philadelphia powerfully applies to our lesson. Read the excerpt thoughtfully:

> In the beginning of the contest with Britain when we were sensible of danger, we had daily prayers in this room for the Divine protection. Our prayers, Sir, were heard, and they were graciously answered. …. And have we now forgotten this powerful Friend? Or do we imagine that we no longer need his assistance? I have lived for a long time (81 years), and the longer I live the more convincing proof I see of this truth, that God governs in the affairs of men. And if a sparrow cannot fall to the ground without his notice, is it possible that an empire can rise without his aid? We have been assured, Sir, in the sacred writings, that "Except the Lord build the house, they labour in vain that build it." I firmly believe this, and I also believe that without his concurring aid we shall proceed in this political building no better than the builders of Babel.[6]

Write a one-sentence synopsis of Franklin's point in your own words:

_____

_____

Consider another intriguing quote from Boice's commentary on Psalm 127: "A Latin motto says, *Nisi Dominus Frusta*. It comes from the first words of this psalm and means 'Without the Lord, Frustration.' It is the motto of the city of Edinburgh Scotland, appearing on its crest, and is affixed to the city's official documents."[7]

When was the last time you realized you were wasting your energies? In Latin terms, when was the last time you experienced "Nisi Dominus Frustra"?

_____

The purpose of today's lesson is to help us drop a very pointed phrase from our personal experience: *vain labor*. Stare at those two words long enough to be disturbed by the prospect. Imagine pouring your daily efforts into something completely meaningless. None of us wants our work to be in vain.

God's basic premise in the opening lines of this inspired song is that, whatever the work may be, if He is not in it, it is meaningless. Let's think in terms of the workplace before we see the psalm in a context of family in our next lesson. You might be encouraged to realize that God can be hard at work in our workplace without our earthly boss ever acknowledging it. God can build a company to serve divine purposes right under the unsuspecting nose of an unbelieving owner. The prophet Daniel is a perfect example of a man whose work was blessed even when his workplace was not.

Don't get the idea that all work is meaningless if it's not vocationally and blatantly Christian. The question we need answered is whether or not God is in our labor and indeed initiated it as His own building project. If you're unsure, ask Him to show you in a way you'll readily recognize. Eugene Peterson writes, "The curse of some people's lives is not work, as such, but senseless work, vain work, futile work, work that takes place apart from God. Work that ignores the *if*."[8]

Personalize Peterson's modern translation of "ifs" into your own creative words.

If GOD *doesn't* _____,

I might as well put my efforts into _____. *If* GOD

doesn't guard _____, *I might as well* _____.

Both of the following New Testament segments echo the concept. Read them and record what you believe God is saying personally to you.

John 5:17 _____

John 15:4-5 _____

> "If GOD doesn't build the house, the builders only build shacks. If GOD doesn't guard the city, the night watchman might as well nap."
>
> Psalm 127:1,
> The Message

Let's spend our remaining moments on Psalm 127:2. In one phrase, what you think this verse is saying?

I don't know what you wrote, but I'll tell you something Psalm 127:2 keeps saying to me: Get some sleep! Under divine inspiration the psalmist tells us that work done while we need to be sleeping is energy burned in vain. A body needs sleep. I almost heard an audible "Amen!" So, if you believe it so readily, why aren't you getting it?

Maybe you are among the few who are getting a proper amount of sleep most of the time. If so, snooze while the rest of us get a stern talking-to. An overwhelming number of Americans are sleep deprived, including yours truly. Some of us have physiological and sociological reasons like pregnancy (not me), young children to care for (not me), and hormonal changes that come with middle age (me!).

Even if we have good reasons like these, we can't just go on and on with very little sleep. We need to seek some solutions! Much of the time, overwork, stress, and anxiety rob exhausted people of sleep. The risks of continued sleep deprivation suggest that whatever reasons we have are probably not good enough. One CNN report says, "Fatigue is dangerous. A growing collection of research indicates that America's sleep problems have reached epidemic proportions, and may be the country's number-one health problem."[9] Sleep deprivation is a problem that leads to all sorts of other problems. Some of them you've experienced personally. And so have I.

Did you happen to think of *irritability?* Don't you know that God sometimes wants to put us down for a nap like a cranky baby? Another report says that sleep deprivation can have some of the same hazardous effects as being drunk. Drivers are especially vulnerable. Researchers found that people who drive after being awake for 17 to 19 hours performed worse than those with a blood alcohol level of .05 percent. ... The study said 16 to 60 percent of road accidents involve sleep deprivation.[10]

Consistent lack of sleep has also been linked to weaker immune systems. One report states that "those who sleep fewer than six hours a night don't live as long as those who sleep seven hours or more."[11]

I'll conclude today's lesson on the futility of godless work and little sleep with one last motivation to call it a day at a decent hour and get some rest. Everything looks better in morning light. I can be undone and frustrated about something at night, but if I'll get down on my knees beside my bed and offer it to God, when I awaken, the sunrise invariably casts a whole new light on the situation. I don't doubt you've had the same experience.

Today's lesson in a mathematical nutshell?

Godless labor + little sleep = a futile expenditure of energy

Work where God works; then rest, Dear Solomon, "for so he giveth his beloved sleep" (Ps. 127:2, KJV).

viewer guide

He Surrounds His People

We are devoting three sessions to the Pilgrim Feasts because they hold such important associations with the Psalms of Ascent. In session 2 we talked about the first Pilgrim Feast on Israel's biblical calendar: the Feast of Unleavened Bread. Today we'll turn our attentions to the second Pilgrim Feast: the Feast of _____, which occurred in the early summer.

Read Deuteronomy 16:9-12 and consider the following explorations of Israel's Feast of Weeks.

1. The Feast of Weeks (Hebrew *Shavuot*) derives its name from the _____

   _____, separating it from the Feast of Firstfruits. Its commemoration

   on the fiftieth day earned it the Greek name of _____.

2. The Feast of Weeks much later became associated with the _____

   _____ _____ _____ at Sinai (*Ex. 19:1*).

3. The Feast of Weeks was a time for _____

   their _____ _____.

4. The Feast of Weeks was a time for _____ _____.

- Generous _____

- Generous _____ —A Bible commentary describes the freewill

  offering of the Israelites at the Feast of Weeks as "a freewill,

  _____ tribute of gratitude to God for His temporal

  _____ *(see Deut. 16:9-12).*

5. The Feast of Weeks was also called the _____ _____

  _____ _____ *(Ex. 23:16).*

- Corporate significance: Acts 2:41. The specific timing of this event on Pentecost
  offers little doubt that God intended a highly significant feast of harvest.

- Personal significance: Galatians 6:9-10. In *The Feasts of the Lord* we are told
  that "because of the commandment to count, the time period from Firstfruits to
  Shavuot is known as *Sefirah*,"[1] a Hebrew word meaning *counting*.

1. Ken Howard and Marvin Rosenthal, *The Feasts of the Lord*, (Nashville: Thomas Nelson, 1997), 90.

Week Four
A Fruitful Vine

Day One: A Heritage From the Lord
Day Two: Enjoy the Blessing
Day Three: Olive Shoots Around Your Table
Day Four: They Have Not Prevailed
Day Five: To Be Heard

Principal Questions

1. What do you think Psalm 127:1 conveys regarding family?

2. What actions incur divine blessing?

3. What is the point of Christ's parable in Luke 19:21-27?

4. What does Isaiah 49:25 tell us our Defender will do?

5. How would you summarize Psalm 129:5-8 in one sentence?

Day One

A Heritage from the Lord

Today as we set both feet on the eighth step in our Psalms of Ascent we'll view Psalm 127 in the context of family.

Please read the entire psalm in either translation offered on week 3, day 5; then list everything it says involving family.

_____

_____

_____

TODAY'S TREASURE

"Sons are indeed a heritage from the LORD, children, a reward."
Psalm 127:3, HCSB

Today we talk about family because our text demands it. Before we do, however, I'd like to minister to those without children. I've been asked if I will ever write a series on marriage and children. Though at some point I probably will, my hesitation has been the participants without children. To some who deeply desire children and have struggled with infertility, the subject matter is like salt in a wound. Others have waited faithfully for God to bring them a spouse, but that life mate still doesn't appear in the picture. My love and respect for every woman God has allowed me to serve makes me cringe a little when I know I'm about to teach something that could be painful.

If you allow me the privilege, I'd like to say something to you from the beginning: You do not have to have physical children to do some effective parenting. Recall how often the apostle Paul referred to Timothy as his "son," though their only blood relationship was in Christ. The early church often used family terminology.

How did Christ blow the doors off our concept of family (Matt. 12:46-50)?

_____

_____

At my home church, we have often celebrated "Mother's and Others" Day with a special banquet. Attendees either bring their literal mothers or daughters or someone *like* a mother or daughter to them. I brought a woman who has been like a second mother to me for 20 years. Miss Mary Helen did not give birth to me, but she is undoubtedly a mother figure. She is my beloved "other." As well, I have a couple of young women who are almost like blood daughters to me. Amanda and Melissa view them much like sisters. Further, my daughters have some women around my age that pour maternal love and advice into their lives. None of these "others" are meant to supplant actual mothers and daughters. They're meant to enhance lives in ways we wouldn't want to miss.

I am very maternal and having an empty nest has been hard for me. As my mom said, I could mother a fence post. A lot of young women need some extra mothering so we can make a good pair. In fact, I've realized along the way that some of what I'm doing in this writing ministry is mothering. Get the picture? Then see yourself in it. Are you aching to mother? Somebody out there needs an "other."

If you already have an "other," whether a mother or daughter figure, describe her place in your life.

Glance back at Psalm 127:1 and see the "house" in terms of family. In Scripture, building a house means more than stacking bricks. It refers to a family line. The house of Keith Moore, biblically speaking, is not an address but a group of people. Our grandson, Jackson, is of the house of Keith Moore just like his mom. Our son-in-law, Curt, is a vital part of the house of Keith Moore, but he will also have his own house. Psalm 127:1 applies to what we think of sociologically as a home. In our previous lesson, we looked at this Scripture in terms of laboring in the workplace.

What do you think Psalm 127:1 conveys regarding family?

I am thankful that Christ was a carpenter by trade. Though He does all things well and every honorable form of work originates in Him, His vocational specialty appears to be construction. Even now He is preparing a place for us so that we'll have the perfect house to occupy when we get to heaven (John 14:2-3). Thank goodness, Christ is fully capable of multitasking because I never cease needing home improvements. My home once needed repairing so badly I thought God was going to have to take a wrecking ball to it and rebuild it from scratch. Since that time God has kept us on a perpetual remodeling contract.

Perhaps your home has been like ours—built on human strength or the pitiful lack of it. Either approach turns out to be in vain. Maybe God wasn't invited from the start to invade every part of your family life and you have suffered the consequences. Maybe you feel like much of your home is in shambles. I've been there too. You can't imagine how hopeless mine looked at times. In desperation I cried out over and over to the only dependable home builder I knew, asking Him to come to the rescue. At times I felt like He was late to work, but little by little I began to see His hand, pouring some new foundation and tearing down walls the enemy had tried to erect between members of my family. Later Keith began to cry out too, and miracles started unfolding. Life between my man and me will retain challenges while we keep an address on this earth, but the difference between our past and our present is monumental. We are not the same people.

Do you need to know today that Christ still specializes in home improvements? O yes O no Without saying too much, write out a few places you'd like to see God perform some much needed repairs.

_____

_____

> Be careful not to expect your marriage, parenting, or even your singleness to be exactly like someone else's.

As you continue to pray, trust and look for signs of His work in your family, keep in mind that Christ is a custom builder. Your home is not going to look exactly like mine and vice versa. Be careful not to expect your marriage, parenting, or even your singleness to be exactly like someone else's. I had to get out of my head that I wanted Keith to be a husband just like _____. Keith is his own man in Christ, and I've been much happier since I accepted his uniqueness. Likewise, he has accepted mine.

Free Christ to be your custom builder. Let Him tell you how He wants your house to look instead of the other way around. He alone has the blueprint.

Let's spend the remainder of the time looking at Psalm 127:3-5. If you are a parent only of daughters like I am, you may be a little offended by the gender terminology regarding sons. Keep in mind that in ancient culture the benefit of sons was primarily practical. They performed physical labor beside their fathers, and when they were grown, they were able to help protect and defend the family and its property. Industry and electronics have transformed our once agrarian culture into a work force where women also make large contributions, making the gender reference in Psalm 127 harder for us to grasp. Certainly daughters are also a heritage from the Lord even if they don't carry on the family name when they marry. They too are a great reward, which brings us to a much needed point.

To prepare, please fill in the following blanks based on Today's Treasure (HCSB):

Sons are indeed _____ heritage from the LORD, children, _____ reward.

Note that Psalm 127:3 does not say sons are *the* heritage from the Lord and children *the* reward. God grants us heritage in numerous ways. His rewards come to us in various forms. Do a word study of the terms *heritage* and *reward* using a Bible concordance and you'll see what I mean. Psalm 127:3 does not mean we are not rewarded by God if we are childless. We may be rewarded bountifully in other areas we've not yet fully enjoyed because we somehow feel condemned or overlooked because we don't have the reward we want. By no means do I desire to minimize the challenge. I care deeply for you and don't want you to feel unloved, unnoticed, and unrewarded because Scriptures like this one seem to couple blessings with children. Sons are *a* heritage, blessed indeed. But like many of you, as much as I wanted one, I never birthed a son. Children are *a* reward, wonderful indeed! But if you have never had a child, the Bible is not telling you that you somehow are unworthy of reward.

Genesis 15:1 identifies the ultimate reward. What it is? _____

_____

"Like arrows in the hand of a warrior are the sons born in one's youth" (Ps. 127:4, HCSB). Let's meditate on this verse before we conclude. Think of any way sons could be like arrows and write your parallels in this space.

_____

_____

The most intentional parallel is the ability of sons to defend the parent and the parent's property, especially during their aging years. I've never birthed a son, but I have two daughters and one son-in-law. I have learned that any of the three would defend me to the death. Because of what I do vocationally, they have more opportunities than I would prefer. I have to be careful where I aim my beloved "arrows" because they'll shoot before I can count to three.

When Amanda first began to work for me, she was in the loop of a few critical letters directed toward me. We knew we needed to take Amanda out of that loop when she answered one ugly letter rather curtly. After taking up for me with no small passion and sprinkling her comments with remarks like "You don't even know her," she iced the cake with: "I should know—she's my mother." It wasn't funny at the time, but soon we all (except Amanda) laughed our heads off at someone raising the ire of our sweet-natured firstborn. Melissa, on the other hand, begged to take Amanda's job after that happened. She's an arrow begging to be shot at anyone who is ugly to one of her family members. What delight my children are to me! A reward from the Lord!

I can't think of a more appropriate way to end today's lesson than to reflect on a time when someone took the position of "arrow" in your defense. Describe the situation as well as you can without slandering the one who brought the offense.

_____

_____

You see? Whether or not you realize it, your "arrow" was taking the position of the son in Psalm 127:4. That's one of the main points of today's lesson. In the wonderful and worldwide family of God, we have fathers, sons, daughters, mothers, and "others." If we're in Christ, we're blood relatives either way. "Happy is the man who has filled his quiver with them" (v. 5).

Wrap up today's lesson by writing your own version of Psalm 127 and jotting down the main point God taught you through this Psalm of Ascent on your stair graphic. I am absolutely crazy about you. Thanks for having me in your house today. I pray Mr. Home Improvement Himself has done a little remodeling on both our families. After all, who wants to labor in vain? *Nisi Dominus Frusta.*

My Psalm 127

Enjoy the Blessing

I have new faces to picture today as I scribble thoughts to you. I just returned from Moab, Utah where we taped the brief introductions and benedictions to the updated version of *A Woman's Heart*. There in the middle of a land void of cell phones and flush toilets, a few of you hiked up.

The cross-section was wonderfully orchestrated by God. Two were single mid-thirties women who were studying *Beloved Disciple* at a neighborhood church in Salt Lake City. Another was a mom with her man and adorable daughters. Each woman took pictures with a camera. I took pictures with my mind. They asked me to pardon the intrusion. Intrusion? Are you kidding? When I lose touch with you, I need to power down my Bible software. I wouldn't even call the picture two of us took in a Moab ladies' room an intrusion. After all, I was washing my hands by then. And you were right. The light green color of the stall wall did indeed provide a good background. Oh, the joy you bring me!

My worst nightmare is losing touch with fellow sojourners, your stories, needs, and joys. Group travel was the core of ancient pilgrimage. Traveling alone was practically unheard of.

God had His reasons for ordaining encounters with those women in Utah, but I know one reason was for me. When the work is hard, the days are long, and the pressures almost unbearable, God appoints a fresh connect with flesh-and-blood sisters in Christ who are on the same journey. Sisters who, like me, could use some camaraderie. Some encouragement to press on. Some belly laughs. Some directions for the path. And, above all, some living words from a living Christ who is the absolute embodiment of abundant life. May looking down from heaven on this band of merry pilgrims—stressed and pressed though we are—bring Christ sheer delight..

Are you ready to step up to our ninth Psalm of Ascent? We'll put one foot on Psalm 128 today and we'll add the other foot tomorrow. Proceed with approaches 1 and 2: *Say it;* then *work it.*

TODAY'S TREASURE
"How happy is everyone who fears the LORD, who walks in His ways!"
Psalm 128:1, HCSB

PSALM 128 (HCSB)

Blessings for Those Who Fear God
A song of ascents.

1 How happy is everyone who fears the LORD, who walks in His ways!

2 You will surely eat what your hands have worked for. You will be happy, and it will go well for you.

3 Your wife will be like a fruitful vine within your house, your sons, like young olive trees around your table.

4 In this very way the man who fears the LORD will be blessed.

5 May the LORD bless you from Zion, so that you will see the prosperity of Jerusalem all the days of your life,

6 and will see your children's children! Peace be with Israel.

PSALM 128 (The Message)

1 A pilgrim song
All-you who fear GOD, how blessed you are! how happily you walk on his smooth straight road!

2 You worked hard and deserve all you've got coming. Enjoy the blessing! Revel in the goodness!

3 Your wife will bear children as a vine bears grapes, your household lush as a vineyard, The children around your table as fresh and promising as young olive shoots.

4 Stand in awe of God's Yes. Oh, how he blesses the one who fears GOD!

5 Enjoy the good life in Jerusalem every day of your life.

6 And enjoy your grandchildren. Peace to Israel!

I'm just going to spit this out: Anybody who claims the Bible doesn't say we're blessed for obedience is out of their theological mind. Without a doubt blessings come in lots of forms and on sometimes bewildering timetables. But come they do. If you've done many of the Bible studies, you know I don't support a prosperity gospel that claims unwavering health and increasing wealth to all with enough faith. But I do believe that Scripture clearly portrays God as responding to obedience with blessing even today.

PRINCIPAL QUESTION

According to these Scriptures, what are some actions that incur divine blessing?

Luke 11:27-28 _____

John 13:14-17 _____

Romans 10:12 _____

Enjoying the blessing of God is the song on the heart of this Psalm. An excerpt from Boice's commentary states the case. "Blessing is the unifying word of Psalm 128, where in most of our English translations the related words 'blessed,' 'blessings,' and 'bless' occur four times (vv. 1,2,4,5). Only verses 3 and 6 are without it. In Hebrew two rich words are used, *asher* in the first part of the psalm (vv. 1-2) and *barak* in the second part (vv. 4-5)."[1]

As you worked Psalm 128, you no doubt noticed the word *happy*. Some translators resist using such a circumstantial and temporal word. The HCSB is a very sound and formal translation. I'm so glad the translators didn't hesitate to use the word.

I rather like the word *happy* and find it extremely biblical. We touched on the word in Psalm 84:4-5 in our introductory session. Today's psalm invites the topic back to the table. I made the point that even if *happy* is most appropriately connected with circumstances, I'd like the record to show that God has made a tremendous impact on my circumstances. I still have a marriage because Jesus not only impacted my heart but He also impacted the circumstances of my home. How about you?

Has walking with God resulted in a change in your circumstances? If so, how?

PERSONAL QUESTION

The Old Testament versions employing the word happy *have ordinarily translated it from the Hebrew word* asher *(also spelled* esher*) rather than* barak. *How does Genesis 30:13 offer a terrific opportunity to see the word* asher *translated?*

Other English versions instead translate the Hebrew *asher* as "blessed." They can do so accurately because the original term encompasses both, suggesting both a condition (blessed) and a human reaction (happy).

Mind you, this blessed bliss doesn't mean the person doesn't have difficulties or even sorrows. How is Matthew 5:4 proof?

In God's economy even those who mourn are blessed. The Greek word translated "blessed" in Matthew 5:4 beautifully expresses the essence of the blessed life. "Biblically, one is pronounced blessed when God is present and involved in his life. The hand of God is at work directing all his affairs for a divine purpose, and thus, in a sense, such a person lived *coram Deo,* before the face of God."[2] Sometimes the circumstances of our suffering may not change, but the circumstances of our hearts are changed in the midst of them through a keen sense of God's presence and a lively perception of His activity.

Blessedness describes the condition of a person who reveres God, steeps her life in Him, and follows His ways. She doesn't just look to God in spiritual or religious matters. She looks to Him in every matter. He's not just the most important part of her life. He is her life. The result of this divine invasion is that the life operates *overall* at optimum earth-satisfaction, joy, and purpose and without the crushing burdens of self-glory and sin. In other words, her life actually works.

Reflect on that last sentence. How would you define a life that "actually works"?

_____

_____

Let's further explore a life that "works" through the following exercises. Take a good look at the wording of Psalm 128:1 in the HCSB. Those who are characterized in this psalm as happy or blessed are those who do two closely associated things.

What two things mark the blessed person? _____

_____

Hopefully the question was clear enough to lead you to these two answers: Psalm 128 characterizes people as happy or blessed who (1) fear (greatly respect and revere) God and (2) walk in His ways. Tomorrow we're going to consider specific ways God responds to obedience with blessing, but today I hope to prove that tremendous blessings come from the obedience itself. Let me see if I can explain.

First, practicing an appropriate fear of God is a blessing. Trying to be our own god is exhausting. A book by a well-known Oxford professor tries to dispel the "myth" of the existence of God. I felt sorry for the writer. I couldn't help but think what a burden being your own god must be. And without the fear of God and the command to bring Him alone glory, what check would we have on our own self-promotion? Nothing is weightier in the long haul than our insatiable egos. You see, fear of the Lord is actually an important element in a healthy human psyche.

What else is the fear of the Lord according to Isaiah 33:6?

_____

Second, walking in God's ways is its own blessing. I'll give you three examples. First, God commands us to love our enemies. He will bless our willingness to do such a hard thing, but He also insists on the best response for our own mental and emotional health. Holding grudges is a malignancy of the soul that makes us miserable.

Second, God says it is more blessed to give than to receive (see Acts 20:35). Takers are miserable. Learning to give is schooling in joy.

Third, God was right about sex with only our spouse. Sex outside of marriage tears at the fabric of our souls because we form ties that are invariably ripped apart. Yes, we can find healing and restoration in Christ, but the blessing of obedience is best. Sometimes the blessing resides in what we avoided, not just in what we gain.

After four-and-one-half decades of getting to know Jesus, I am utterly convinced that His ways are simply right and walking in His ways will, therefore, always be the right thing in every circumstance. Try as you may, you will never think of a situation in which God's ways aren't best. Hosea 14:9 (HCSB) states the premise perfectly: "Let whoever is wise understand these things, and whoever is insightful recognize them. For the ways of the LORD are right."

Christians have too long been intimidated by the jeers of secular philosophers. God's ways are right. Not only does He declare the way to eternal life; His precepts on personal conduct in the here and now are best. In loving God and then loving others as we love ourselves, we in effect keep the entire law. No other belief system honors the human race like Christianity, despite reputations and claims. We are not oppressed when we fear God and walk in His ways. We, Beloved, are blessed.

Day Three
Olive Shoots Around Your Table

I stood in the bakery aisle yesterday dazed and confused. For the life of me I could not make a move toward one loaf of bread. "Should I get white bread or wheat bread?" I asked myself. Wheat's better for you but I like white on a sandwich, especially on a peanut butter and jelly. Turkey, too, come to think of it. And if I could've made up my mind about white or wheat, I was then faced with the question of thick or thin sliced. And is a store brand as good as a name brand? Most importantly, which one is the freshest? My kids and I like it squashy.

Praise God, I don't always have that much trouble at the grocery store. Yesterday, however, my brain was totally fried. *Blonder Than She Pays to Be* had made all the decisions she could make in one day. So there I stood, paralyzed somewhere between the buns and the fruit juice. At least five patrons wearing smarty pants walked up and grabbed their loaves as if they were in the dough-know. I was in the mood to smack somebody with a firm pack of day-old. Thankfully, I didn't have the energy to give in to it. Finally, Keith finished up on the dog food aisle and came back and found me in a dead stare at the baked goods. "Need some help?"

"Yep."

"How about this one?"

"That will be fine. I don't even care. I hate bread."

TODAY'S TREASURE
"Your wife will be like a fruitful vine within your house, your sons, like young olive trees around your table"
Psalm 128:3, HCSB

When I'm faced with a relational or social decision, I can find my answer pretty quickly by asking myself: what respects God most and reflects His ways?

Actually, I love bread, but loving bread was obviously too much for me yesterday. Ever felt like that? Ever found yourself unable to make the most trivial decision? We spent our entire lesson yesterday on Psalm 128:1. We learned that God blesses those who revere Him and walk in His ways. Those two precepts simplify a multitude of life decisions for us. So often when I'm faced with a relational or social decision, I can find my answer pretty quickly by asking myself: what respects God most and reflects His ways? The inquiry doesn't help much with bread, but it helps with a host of far more important dilemmas like how I'm going to act in a conflict, how I'm going to answer an insult, and, movie lover that I am, whether I'm going to buy that ticket.

Write Hosea 14:9 (HCSB) from day 2 as a great reminder as we prepare to put both feet on Psalm 128.

_____

_____

_____

Yesterday we talked about ways reverence and obedience are blessings in and of themselves. God's ways are always right and His commands always have positive effects. They protect not only His supremacy but our humanity. Today we see beyond the immediate benefits that God blesses those who fear Him and walk in His ways.

Read from day 2 Psalm 128:1-4,6 in either version. How does it depict blessing?

_____

_____

You've noticed the continuing theme of family in Psalm 127. One of the beautifully constructed elements of the Psalms of Ascent is how almost every step carries on some dimension of the previous one. They were never meant to be autonomous but are interconnected by certain themes. Jerusalem is one of them. Traveling together is another. The core of any group on pilgrimage was family. The Psalms of Ascent would be incomplete without references to family since the family unit and the concept of lineage had been the backbone of the nation since Abraham and Sarai were first promised an heir. The type of blessings Christ promised those under the New Covenant widen the table considerably, making room for many chairs. You have to know that I feel strongly about drawing a New Testament application if I'm foregoing the temptation to build an entire lesson on the joy of grandchildren.

Consider Eugene Peterson's broader view of the family in Psalm 128. "The illustration is, as we would expect, conditioned by Hebrew culture, in which the standard signs of happiness were a wife who had many children and children who gathered

and grew around the table: fruitful vine and olive shoots. This illustration is just that, an example that we need not reproduce exactly in order to experience blessing. (We, for instance, don't try to have as many children as possible—or try to get them to stay home for all their lives!) But the meaning is still with us: Blessing has inherent in it the power to increase."[3]

Meditate on the last line. The concept it describes is the heart of today's lesson. Underscore it by completing this sentence based on Peterson's quote:

"But the meaning is still with us: _____

_____ ."

Let's see if we can discover in the following Scriptures some blessings to pilgrims under the New Covenant (Luke 22:20; 2 Cor. 3:6) that echo those described in Psalm 128 to children of God under the Old Covenant.

Read Genesis 1:27-28. What was God's first command to Adam and Eve?

_____

_____

How did God say something similar to Abram, God's chosen father of Israel?

Genesis 15:5 _____

Genesis 17:6 _____

What is Christ called in 1 Corinthians 15:45? _____

What was Christ's final face-to-face command to His disciples (Matt. 28:19)?

_____

Circle the term the psalmist used in Psalm 128:3 to describe the wife.

a bride adorned for her husband   a mother to all   a fruitful vine

Read John 15:1-8 and answer the following questions:

What terminology did Christ use for Himself (v. 1)? _____

What did Christ call His disciples (v. 5)? _____

Why does God prune branches (John 15:2)? _____

What must the branch do to bear fruit (v. 4)? _____

How is our Father glorified (v. 8)? _____

John 15:16 is comprised of two sentences. Write the first sentence:

_____

_____

God's creative consistency in His Word thrills me. Consistency without creativity can be monotony. Creativity without consistency is fragmented. An author who can't make up his mind leaves his reader confused and feeling pointless.

In my brief study of the Koran, I marveled at the contrast to the Bible. In comparison, the Koran is disjointed and reads like scattered puzzle pieces that can't find their fit. The Word of God, on the other hand, is a compilation of 66 books God breathed through multiple human authors resulting in one superlative theme: redemption.

From Genesis to Revelation, the Bible is the story of God's pursuit of fallen man and God's willingness to make the ultimate sacrifice to win him. It is an unsurpassed masterpiece. I find tremendous security in knowing that amid human turmoil and failure, God doesn't keep changing His mind and starting over. I need to know that everything is still going according to the plan set before time began. Don't you?

With perfect consistency, multiplied in both the Old Testament and the New, God calls His own to be fruitful. With marvelous creativity He transitioned from the Old Covenant bloodline of Abraham into the New Testament bloodline of Christ. We are a spiritual family line.

We see another creative transition in contrasting the metaphors of Psalm 128 and John 15. In the psalm the fruitful vine is the wife. In the New Testament segment, the Vine is Christ Himself. Don't miss the fact that the followers of Christ, later called His Bride, comprise the branches. The branches as uninterrupted extensions of the Vine is the point of Christ's teaching. The Bride of Christ is still the one ultimately commanded to increase and to bear much fruit. I want you to see something very important as we draw our thoughts on Psalm 128 to an end.

PRINCIPAL QUESTION

Keeping everything we've talked about in mind, please read Christ's parable in Luke 19:21-27. What is the point of this parable?

_____

The word I'm about to share came as a fresh revelation to me. When Christ called His Bride (His church) to be fruitful, and through its fruitfulness, to multiply, He wasn't just issuing a great idea or even an invitation. He was issuing a command. God not only enables increase but He also expects it. What we read of Christ's final face-to-face words to His disciples in Matthew 28:19 is not called *The Great Permission*. It's called *The Great Commission*.

Christ chose and appointed *you* to go and bear fruit—fruit that will last. He placed His Spirit within you the moment you received Him as Savior. He anointed you and equipped you with spiritual gifts. He means for you to use them with great effectiveness in the body of Christ. He has given you life experiences intended to turn into testimonies and ministries that help make the Savior irresistible to the seeker.

Christ did not issue you permission to bear much fruit. He issued you a commission. What do you sense Him saying personally to you right now?

PERSONAL QUESTION

As Psalm 128 promises, your fear of the Lord and willingness to walk in obedience to this command will most assuredly result in blessing. You see, in Eugene Peterson's words, "the meaning is still with us: Blessing has inherent in it the power to increase." Write your name here: "_____, be fruitful and multiply."[4]

Thank you for your hard work today, Sweet One. Don't think for a moment Christ doesn't notice your diligence. Your study life is a huge investment in your fruitfulness. Put the finishing touches on the lesson by filling in your stair graphic with the main idea you received from God through our ninth Psalm of Ascent. Then write your own version. I love you.

My Psalm 128

Day Four

They Have Not Prevailed

My mom loved retelling a story of something sassy I said when I was four. I heard someone say, "If you sprinkle salt on a bird's tail, you can catch it." I took it literally and proceeded to empty an entire carton of Morton's salt trying to catch every bird that lit in our yard. From our kitchen window, Mom could see my grimy face covered with sweat and streaming with tears of frustration. When she could stand the sight no longer, she stopped me, got down on her knees and said, "Bethie, the saying is a riddle. It just means if you can get that close to a bird, you can probably catch it. God made birds to be free."

Miffed with her answer, I retreated to the house, slammed the door, and flung my Barbie dolls all over the floor. When told to pick them up, I announced sassily, "I will not! God made me to be free." My mom felt her own freedom to give me a spanking.

TODAY'S TREASURE

"Since my youth they have often attacked me, but they have not prevailed against me."
Psalm 129:2, HCSB

I've thought of that story many times and wondered if Christ got a twinkle in His eye over the entire interchange on freedom. After all, it would become my God-given life's passion. Don't you think He looked with great interest and affection on encounters in your own young life that bore hints of your future in Him? I have a hard time picturing Christ unsentimental about those kinds of things.

All those years ago I was right about one thing: God made me to be free just as He did you. I couldn't have been more mistaken about another: Freedom never comes through disobedience. Today's lesson is a reminder. Let's take the first step onto our tenth Psalm of Ascent. You'll find the two translations on the next page. After you *say it* and *work it,* please return to this point of the lesson and continue.

The psalmist made dividing the chapter into two parts easy. We will consider the first four verses today, centering on the oppressed. On day 5 we'll discuss the last four verses, turning the table on the oppressor.

The same Hebrew transliteration *sarar* is translated "oppressed" in the NIV, "attacked" in the HCSB, "persecuted" in the NASB, and "afflicted" in the ESV. Strong's dictionary defines *sarar* as: "to be an enemy, adversary; to bind up ... hamper, oppress, be in distress; vex, besiege."[5] The word picture illustrating oppression is a force pressing or pressuring us so far down or cramping us into such a knot that we feel too constrained to exercise our God-given rights and effectiveness.

PSALM 129 (HCSB)

Protection of the Oppressed
A song of ascents.

1 Since my youth they have often
   attacked me—let Israel say—

2 Since my youth they have often attacked me,
   but they have not prevailed against me.

3 Plowmen plowed over my back; they made
   their furrows long.

4 The LORD is righteous; He has cut the ropes
   of the wicked.

5 Let all who hate Zion be driven back in disgrace.

6 Let them be like grass on the rooftops, which
   withers before it grows up

7 and can't even fill the hands of the reaper or
   the arms of the one who binds sheaves.

8 Then none who pass by will say, "May the
   LORD's blessing be on you." We bless you
   in the name of the LORD.

PSALM 129 (NIV)

A song of ascents.

1 They have greatly oppressed me from my youth—
   let Israel say—

2 they have greatly oppressed me from my youth,
   but they have not gained the victory over me.

3 Plowmen have plowed my back and made their
   furrows long.

4 But the LORD is righteous; he has cut me free from
   the cords of the wicked.

5 May all who hate Zion be turned back in shame.

6 May they be like grass on the roof, which withers
   before it can grow;

7 with it the reaper cannot fill his hands, nor the
   one who gathers fill his arms.

8 May those who pass by not say, "The blessing
   of the LORD be upon you; we bless you in the
   name of the LORD."

Psalm 18:19 paints a very different picture of life with God as our Deliverer.
What image does it use to contrast with oppression?

_____

It's testimony time. In what way would you say God has brought you out
of oppression into a spacious place?

_____

_____

I wish I could sit down and hear you personally relate your answer. One day we'll have time to do just that, Beloved. In the meantime, the enemy, the world system, and our own flesh try to convince us that we're free when we are out from under authority and can do as we please. The Bible and life experience teach us something completely different. Only under the umbrella of God's trustworthy, *for-us* authority do we find our spacious place. You might say these words out loud: *Because God is gracious, His place is spacious.* With word pictures in play, consider the following points about oppression:

When oppression begins in our youth (v. 1), one oppressor can ultimately turn into many. Notice the reference to multiple oppressors: "They have greatly oppressed me since my youth" (v. 1, NIV). Since I have no memory of life before victimization, oppressive people and forces seemed normal to me. I continued to unintentionally work myself into one oppressive relationship after another. Some appeared almost ideal at first and I'd think I'd broken the cycle. Sooner or later, however, most of my close relationships proved unhealthy, particularly the love interests.

Keep in mind, you don't have to be abused when you're young to develop an oppression addiction. I have friends who were oppressed by parents bound by religious legalism, robbing them of joy and freedom in Christ. Those friends equated authority with domination; and rebellion was the great escape. The inevitable result was another form of oppression wearing a different outfit.

Anything we've continued to battle from our youth is habitual enough to require Christ's healing work. Only He can clarify our clouded belief systems. Otherwise, the cycle will never break. One oppressor—be it a self-destructive parent or neighborhood bully—with enough impact on our young, formative years can lead to a string of other oppressors.

Read Psalm 71:17-18. How can this contrasting context of "from my youth" counteract the oppression many of us may have endured from our youth?

_____

_____

_____

Each individual reacts to the same oppression differently.

Each individual reacts to the same oppression differently. Psalm 129 begins with the entire people of Israel then immediately switches to the individual. Loren Crowe writes, "The language of Psalm 129, with the exceptions of vv. 1 and 5, is entirely individual."[6] What is true of individuals within a nation under oppressive influences is also true of individuals within a close unit like a family or workplace. I know a family of six children who each reacted differently to the conflicts and emotional abuses of their parents. One escaped through substance abuse. Another turned to a cult. Still another tried perfectionism. Another tried to become the peacekeeper, when as Scripture so poignantly says, "there was no peace" to keep (see Ezek. 13:16). Each of us has a different personality mix and develops different coping mechanisms.

Think of an oppressive situation you endured with others. How did you react to it or cope with it, particularly in your own human nature?

_____

_____

Think of another person who shared the same environment and had a completely different reaction. Without naming the person, describe it.

_____

_____

We may react differently but make no mistake, we're all reacting. Hurtful situations hurt, and if they don't, something worse than pain has occurred. We've grown callous and cold. One common reaction for many of us is to develop a victim mentality, bringing us to the next point of consideration.

People oppressed from youth often grow up to let strong personalities walk all over them. That's the word picture sketched by Psalm 129:3.

Fill in the following blanks according to the HCSB:

"Plowmen plowed _____;

they made their _____."

Been there? Me too.

Read Isaiah 51:22-23 carefully and thoughtfully. What does verse 23 say about the backs of some of God's children?

_____

Beloved, we can offer people our love without offering them our backs. We can offer them our compassion without offering them our backs. As you and I have taken our places on our faces, God, the righteous Father, never walks on our backs. Christ gave His back to scourging so we, the rightful recipients of such agony, could instead receive dignity. "And by His stripes we are healed" (Isa. 53:5, NKJV).

On our faces, we now humble ourselves under His mighty hand that He may lift us up in due time (see 1 Pet. 5:6). Glance back at the good news in Isaiah 51:22. Here we're told that the Sovereign LORD defends His people. The wider context suggests His defense follows our heart's return to Him and our cry of need, even if our own idolatry, unbelief, or rebellion has led to our oppression.

What does Isaiah 49:25 tell us our Defender will do? _____

_____

PRINCIPAL
QUESTION

Glance back at either of our texts of Psalm 129. I love the *Word Biblical Commentary* translation of the Hebrew in verse 4: "Yahweh is loyal."[7]

How much does God's loyalty mean to you and why?

_____

_____

_____

Comprehending God's loyalty to us and consciously leaving all vindication to Him is crucial if you and I don't want to inadvertently go from being oppressed to being an oppressor. If we don't allow God to heal our hearts, minds, and habits, we will either continue to allow people to walk all over us or we'll become people who walk all over them.

Perhaps you've had an oppressive background but you're inclined to think you don't do either one. If you've never sought Christ's healing, please allow me to gently suggest that people who walk on others rarely if ever recognize it. If we've been oppressed from our youth, without a deep work of God, we're almost certainly reacting one way or the other.

The best news of Psalm 129 is heralded in verse 2. Complete the following sentence accordingly: Since my youth they have often attacked me,

_____

Did they prevail? I'm not asking if they never got in a good hit. I've been pummeled. Sure, our oppressors have won some battles, but they will not win this war. Has Satan gotten the victory he sought? I don't think so. The fact that your Bible is open and you're seeking to walk with God is proof.

Let me tell you how the scenario depicted in Psalm 129 backfires on the Evil One. When oppressors have walked all over us, the plowed up ground left by their feet can become a fertile place for God to cultivate some seed. Make no mistake, desperation digs a hole where a tree gets planted, whether the fruit it bears is good or bad.

When we begin to see our value in Christ and go to our faces, giving our backs to Him rather than to others, if we'll take Him at His Word, He'll sow His seed into those furrows. In time, an oak of righteousness will grow, "a planting of the LORD for the display of his splendor" (Isa. 61:3, NIV). Its branches will give hope to the hurting, shade to the children, and aggravation to the Devil.

He just can't shake enough salt on our tail feathers to catch us. God made us to be free.

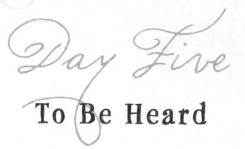

To Be Heard

Today we stand with both feet on our tenth step. On day four we saw the psalm as a parallel to our lives, but we'll miss its wonder if we fail to also view it from Israel's standpoint. The nation of Israel was born after much time, many doubts, missteps, and birth pangs. The latter half of Genesis chronicles Israel's infancy. The Book of Exodus, then, unfolds the scroll of her troubled youth with an entirely new and worrisome picture:

> "A new king, who had not known Joseph, came to power in Egypt. He said to his people, 'Look, the Israelite people are more numerous and powerful than we are. Let us deal shrewdly with them; otherwise they will multiply further, and if war breaks out, they may join our enemies, fight against us, and leave the country.' So the Egyptians assigned taskmasters over the Israelites to oppress them with forced labor. They built Pithom and Rameses as supply cities for Pharaoh. But the more they oppressed them, the more they multiplied and spread so that the Egyptians came to dread the Israelites. They worked the Israelites ruthlessly and made their lives bitter with difficult labor in brick and mortar, and in all kinds of fieldwork. They ruthlessly imposed all this work on them" (Ex. 1:8-14, HCSB).

TODAY'S TREASURE
"Then none who pass by will say, 'May the LORD's blessing be on you.'"
Psalm 129:8, HCSB

The nation's oppression by the Egyptians was only the first of many and the reason why Psalm 129:1-2 could claim with perfect accuracy, "They have greatly oppressed me from my youth—let Israel say—they have greatly oppressed me from my youth" (NIV). Looking back on the nation's history, the wonder is that they could make the next statement: "but they have not prevailed against me" (v. 2, HCSB).

James Montgomery Boice reminds us that "the Jews are the longest-enduring distinct ethnic people on the planet. They have been slandered, hated, persecuted, expelled, pursued, and murdered throughout their long existence, but they have survived intact."[8] Derek Kidner offers this remark concerning Psalm 129: "Whereas most nations tend to look back on what they have achieved, Israel reflects here on what she has survived."[9]

Frederick the Great, the king of Prussia, became skeptical and unbelieving, largely due to Voltaire, the famous French rationalist skeptic. The king challenged his chaplain about the truthfulness of the Bible. He said, " 'If your Bible is really true, it ought to be capable of very brief proof … If your Bible is really from God, you should be able to demonstrate the fact simply. Forget long arguments. Give me the proof of the Bible's inspiration in a word.' … The chaplain answered, "Israel," your Majesty.' Frederick, the story goes, was silent."[10]

Keith and I occasionally look back on some of the obstacles and great difficulties we each encountered in our young years and marvel that to God's great glory alone we made it at all. Sometimes life is so atrocious that surviving is its own great achievement and a strange proof of sorts that God must exist.

Based on your life or someone else's (including any historical figure), can you think of an example when survival was in itself a crowning achievement?

PRINCIPAL QUESTION

The remainder of our lesson will center on the second half of the psalm as we shift the focus of the lens from the oppressed to the oppressor. Glance back at either text in our previous lesson and write a one-sentence synopsis of Psalm 129:5-8.

Scholars call this portion of Psalm 129 an *imprecatory psalm,* or one that invites or invokes judgment, evil or even some kind of curse on someone or something. According to *Hard Sayings of the Bible,* 18 psalms possess some element of imprecation or cursing, and a total of 65 verses within them give imprecatory voice.[11]

Psalm 5:8-12 houses the first imprecatory segment in the psalms. Read the segment and list each specific imprecation.

Some theologians insist that imprecatory psalms must not have been inspired. They assume God can't bless such requests. Inspired requests don't necessarily receive an automatic yes. Case in point, in the garden of Gethsemane, Christ prayed for the cup of suffering and death to pass by Him if God willed. The request was inspired and yet a different answer transpired.

Hebrews 5:7 says Jesus "offered up prayers and petitions with loud cries and tears to the one who could save him from death, and he was heard because of his reverent submission" (NIV). Everything Christ did and said was inspired because He was and is completely God. Yet because He exists to do the will of His Father, He could make a divine request that didn't invoke an automatic yes. We are implicitly told that God heard Christ's requests even though one of them did not receive an affirmative answer. The implication is that sometimes an important part of praying is simply being *heard.*

The heart of prayer is communication and not just receiving what we ask. Hence, imprecatory psalms. Sometimes God lets His children blow off some steam.

Don't get me wrong. We certainly need to be careful with what we say and what we request, but the prayers of these songs came from hearts tipping over with honest emotion and poured out before a wise God. One might argue that God allowed these kinds of requests in the Old Testament but New Testament believers are taught to love their enemies and pray for those who mistreat them. You may be surprised to know that God set up many similar ground rules for the treatment of others under both covenants.

Look up each of the following and write in your own words what God commanded.

Exodus 23:4-5 _____

_____

Leviticus 19:16-18 _____

_____

_____

Proverbs 24:17-18 _____

_____

_____

I absolutely love Nahum M. Sarna's description of the psalms. Meditate on the words of this Jewish scholar in light of our discussion on imprecatory prayers:

> "In the Law and the Prophets, God reaches out to man. The initiative is His. The message is His. He communicates, we receive. Our God-given free will allows us to be receptive, to be accepting, to turn a deaf ear, to reject. In the Psalms, human beings reach out to God. The initiative is human. The language is human. We make an effort to communicate. He receives; he chooses to respond or not, according to His inscrutable wisdom. He gives his assent or withholds it. In the Psalms, the human soul extends itself beyond its confining, sheltering, impermanent house of clay. It strives for contact with the Ultimate Source of all life. It gropes for an experience of the divine Presence. The biblical psalms are essentially a record of the human quest for God. Hence, the variety of forms in which the ancient psalmists expressed themselves, reflective of the diverse and changing moods that possessed them as they do all human beings. In short, the psalms constitute a revealing portrayal of the human condition."[12]

The heart of prayer is communication.

Considering Sarna's comments, why do you think God allowed imprecatory psalms on the pages of Holy Writ?

_____

_____

PERSONAL QUESTION

When have you needed to be "heard" by God more than you needed Him to give you what you momentarily might have wanted?

_____

_____

Hard Sayings of the Bible makes a fascinating point: "David was the author of far more imprecatory psalms than anyone else," but ironically, "David exhibited just the opposite of a vindictive or revengeful spirit in his own life."[13]

Think carefully. Why do you think this was true? _____

_____

Maybe David's actions echoed Romans 12:17-21. Vengeance is God's right alone. The man after God's own heart refused to be overcome by evil. Rather, he overcame evil with good. Still, he felt free to be heard in his strong but momentary emotion.

Years ago I had a strange encounter with God I've never forgotten. I was recounting to Him for surely the one-hundredth time my devastation and confusion over a betrayal. I'd never really perceived a discernable reaction from God before, which is probably why I continued to press the point. Suddenly I sensed God's interrupting me with words that were inaudible to my ears but clear to my heart: "Beth, what would you like for Me to do with her? Name it." I knew in a strange sense He was inviting me to name her punishment. I was appalled … and of course He knew I would be. I thought over my own track record and recalled God's strong warnings about judging others and responded with tears, "I want You to have mercy on her." Strangely, the case was closed after that.

I never brought the hurt up again to God with an imprecatory attitude. My petition shifted to blessing. The question of whether or not God would have done what I asked is irrelevant. He knew He had silenced me. I was "heard" until He'd heard enough.

I hope our study of this brief compilation of psalms is stirring your heart with fresh wonder. It is mine. God is wonderfully mysterious—so infinite, complex, and so completely "other than" us that we can never completely figure out His system. As for our system, on the other hand, God's task is utterly simple. As our prayers ascend to His throne, He hears our mouths and then tunes His ear to the frequency of our hearts.

Conclude today by writing your own version of Psalm 129 and filling in your stair graphic.

My Psalm 129

viewer guide

A Fruitful Vine

Read Deuteronomy 16:13-17.

Consider the following distinctive elements of the Feast of Tabernacles and their significance during the time Christ traveled to Jerusalem to celebrate.

1. The great invitation to _____ (*Deut. 16:15*)

2. The strong emphasis on _____ (*Ps. 118:24-26*)

• Compare Leviticus 23:40 and Matthew 21:1-9.

• See Matthew 17:4.

3. The beauty of the _____ (*2 Chron. 5:3*). See John 8:12.

4. The celebration of _____ _____. See Isaiah 12:3;
   then John 7:37-39.

   Not coincidentally, Christ made the offer of " _____

   of _____ _____."

5. The coinciding name: the Feast of _____
   (*John 14:2-3; Rev. 7:9-10*)

PILO

HO

Week Five
My Hope Is in the Lord

POST CARD

Principal Questions

1. According to Colossians 2:15, who has been made the public spectacle?

2. What else is with the Lord besides unfailing love (Ps. 130:3, NIV)?

3. At first glance, what does Psalm 131:1 say to you?

4. What do Deuteronomy 1:31; 32:18; Isaiah 46:3-4; 49:15; 66:13 tell us about specific ways God parents?

5. What is the ark called in Psalm 132:7?

משנה סדר נשים
(Seder Nashim)

Day One

If You Kept a Record

I was pecking away at our Bible study when I got a call from Melissa. Before I could say, "Good morning, Sweetie!" she said cheerfully but abruptly, "Pray for me on the phone quick, Mom! The battery on my cell is about to die!" I didn't even have to ask her what to pray about. She's taking final exams in a brutal master's degree program. After I prayed for her, she squeezed in the time for a fast, "How are *you*, Mom?" I responded, "Melissa, did you know that if the Lord kept a record of sins, no one could stand?" Unexpectedly my voice began to quiver so much that I couldn't get the next Scripture out of my mouth. She took a moment to smile and reflect. "Ah, Mom, you're on a wonderful Psalm of Ascent right now, aren't you?"

Yes, I am. I write to you today with tears burning in my eyes. I realized recently how many times, when introducing a new Psalm of Ascent, I've told you, "This one means so much to me." Or "this is one of my favorites." No wonder God directed me to write on these songs I thought I knew nothing about. Many of them have been like fountains of living Water to this road-weary traveler who detoured too many times into the ditch on her way to Mount Zion. That He still bid me "Come!" is a grace gift beyond comprehension.

I pray the words of our eleventh Psalm of Ascent will mean something profound to you too. So say it and work it now on page 121. Then come back to this page.

I chose a more scholarly second translation over a modern version of this psalm because it demonstrates a distinctive characteristic I don't want you to miss. The writer of Psalm 130 intentionally addressed God by three different Hebrew names.

How are the names translated into English in your second version?

_____   _____   _____

If you'll check the HCSB, you can see the difference between *Yahweh* and *Adonay,* respectively, by the uppercase LORD and the upper- and lower-case Lord. *Yahweh,* also translated "Jehovah," is the covenant name God used to invite Israel into relationship. That *Yahweh* is God's covenant name is all the more significant when you realize it expresses His self-existence, "I am who I am," like no other title. He whose existence depends on nothing and no one created man for relationship out of His pure desire to do so. *Adonay* (also spelled *Adonai),* on the other hand, refers to God as Master and Superior, as Sovereign Ruler over all.

TODAY'S TREASURE

"If you, O LORD, kept a record of sins, O LORD, who could stand?"
Psalm 130:3, NIV

PSALM 130 (HCSB)

Awaiting Redemption
A song of ascents.
1 Out of the depths I call to You, LORD!
2 LORD, listen to my voice; let Your ears be attentive to my cry for help.
3 Lord, if You considered sins, LORD, who could stand?
4 But with You there is forgiveness, so that You may be revered.
5 I wait for the LORD; I wait, and put my hope in His word.
6 I wait for the LORD more than watchmen for the morning—more than watchmen for the morning.
7 Israel, put your hope in the LORD. For there is faithful love with the LORD, and with Him is redemption in abundance.
8 And He will redeem Israel from all its sins.

PSALM 130 (ICC)

Out of the depths I cry unto Thee, YAHWEH.

O hearken to my voice, ADONAY, let Thine ears be attentive to the voice of my supplications.

If iniquities Thou shouldest mark, Yah, who could stand?

For with Thee, ADONAY, is pardon; that (Thy Law) may be revered.
I wait on YAHWEH; my soul doth wait; for His word I hope;

My soul for ADONAY, from morning watch to morning watch.

For with YAHWEH is kindness, and plenteous with Him is ransom:

Inasmuch as He ransometh Israel out of all his iniquities.

Can you think of any reason the psalmist might have addressed God by both titles in this context? No right or wrong answer exists. Imagine you were the psalmist; then offer your thoughts as to why you used both names:

_____

_____

_____

_____

Among many reasons, I think the psalmist approached the Master with respect. He spoke these words to One who could command the earth to crack open like monstrous jaws and swallow sinful man into its depths. Instead, God offers forgiveness. May we bow down in wonder.

The Hebrew reference less familiar to English students is "Yah," also spelled "Jah." This shortened form of the covenant name "Yahweh" is employed many times in the Hebrew Old Testament. You say it every time you use the word, *Hallelujah*, meaning "Praise ye Jah." Here is the part I find most intriguing: "JAH is a shortened form of *Jehovah* … Pronounced "yä," this name signifies, *He is*, and can be made to correspond to I AM, just as *Jehovah* corresponds to the fuller expression I AM THAT I AM."[1]

Review Lockyer's thoughts here:

Jehovah corresponds to _____ .

Jah can correspond to _____ .

What's the big deal? Recollect a few of the "I am" statements of Jesus.

> "John 8:24 makes recognition that Jesus is the 'I am' a matter of eternal life and death: 'You will die in your sins unless you believe that I am.' … That the Jews rightly understood Jesus' claim 'Before Abraham was, I am' (8:58) as a divine claim is evident from their picking up stones to throw at Him. The 'I am' of John 18:5 again suggests more than 'I am the man you are looking for.' Rather Jesus is the 'I am' whose awesome presence forced the guard back and into a posture of reverence."[2]

No wonder Hebrews 11:6 says what it does. Circle the two words Hebrews 11:6 says those who come to God must believe.

> "Without faith it is impossible to please him: for he that cometh to God must believe that he is, and that he is a rewarder of them that diligently seek Him" (Heb. 11:6, KJV).

Faith means believing much more than God exists. Even the demons believe that about Him (Jas. 2:19). I think the deeper meaning of Hebrews 11:6 could be that we must believe that *He is* the *I Am!*

Consider this afresh: the fullness of the Godhead bodily (Col. 2:9, KJV), the very *I Am*, hung on a cross and gave His self-existent life to pay the penalty for your sins. He shed His blood for every one of us. "For all have sinned and fall short of the glory of God" (Rom. 3:23).

Recently I was in an old-fashioned revival service with my friend, Dr. James MacDonald. After he vividly described repentance, he asked if anyone in the crowd wanted to come forward and repent. Only a few hundred of the several thousand kept their seat. I couldn't hold back my tears.

My heart aches for those with my kind of past who continue on in their defeat because they think only they have failed. Everything from moral to financial failure smears us with shame long after the poor choice. The silence of the body of Christ leaves people to think no one would understand. I prayed that the sight of so many would remind each repentant soul that we've all sinned and without grace, no one could stand.

Could you or someone you love use the reminder that we've all sinned? If so, why?

_____

_____

Jesus is the author of connection. Satan is the author of isolation. The more our enemy takes us captive, the further we distance ourselves from healthy people. If we remain in captivity long enough, our circle will get smaller and smaller. We'll finally begin to despise (at the very least resent) the few in it with us. Ultimately we feel isolated even from the few until we're left with the feeling that we are entirely alone.

Have you ever experienced this isolation? If so, describe your encounter with it.

_____

_____

Listen carefully: God never disconnects Himself from His children. See for yourself. Read Psalm 139:7-10; then name all the places God accompanies us:

_____

_____

For crying out loud, God is so connected to us, He even shows up where we don't want Him! No matter how ashamed we are for Him to find us in the shape we're in, acknowledging His Presence in our pit is our first step out. "Out of the depths I call to You, LORD!" (Ps.130:1).

Glance back at Today's Treasure. What does the psalmist's rhetorical question convey to us that God does not do?

_____

The metaphor in verse 3 is a "divine storage of sins."[3] Imagine what heaven would be like if, when you get there, God raises the door on your storage unit (mine would be huge) and brings out one memento after another representing each sin. For me, that would not be heaven. It would be a descent into hell.

If my question was clear enough, you wrote, "He keeps no record of sins." Read that sentence again until it finally sinks in. No divine storage unit keeps the record of your sins until you arrive. Yes, we experience earthly consequences and chastisement for our sins, but 1 John 1:9 implicitly tells us, "If we confess our sins, He is faithful and righteous to forgive us our sins and to cleanse us from all unrighteousness" (HCSB). Circle the word "all." That infinitely broad term includes the one thing you keep reliving and grieving.

Beloved, if you're like me, God is not the one keeping the record. You are. You keep playing that record over and over. You may think you're honoring God with misery over your past mistakes, but you're not. Just like I did, you're walking in unbelief—not trusting what He promised to do if you'd repent. Having my eyes opened to this reality several years ago changed my entire view on self-condemnation. It does not honor God.

Read Colossians 2:13-15. How many of our sins did Christ forgive (v. 13)?

What did Christ do with the written code (or law) that testified against us (v. 14)?

PRINCIPAL QUESTION

Too many teachers try to convince us that God will make a public spectacle of us over our sins when we get to heaven. According to Colossians 2:15, who has been made the public spectacle?

As for us, Psalm 32:1-2 says, "How happy is the one whose transgression is forgiven, whose sin is covered! How happy is the man the LORD does not charge with sin, and in whose spirit is no deceit!"

Do you want to honor God with your response to His forgiveness? Then be happy about it! Jump up and down with relief and joy! Elation is one of the things God uses to make nothing worth returning to that sin. You will come to love the feeling of forgiveness and freedom much more than fleshly pleasure. Our enduring misery over our past is one reason we end up going back into the pit. Somewhere deep in our souls we want to punish ourselves and return to what we deserve. Dear One, Christ took what we deserve.

"Happy is the one whose transgression is forgiven!" Go ahead and feel it.

Full Redemption

I often recall something I heard from Florence Littauer, "Of all things beyond salvation, people are most desperate for hope." I know from personal experience. After a terrible season of sin, I would've despaired without biblical hope that I had not destroyed my future. My shattered heart told me I was finished, but as I held my Bible to my chest day after day, surviving on its precepts, I finally accepted that the truth of Scripture trumps every human emotion. In doing so, I put my hope in His Word. A season of sin is not the only thing that can make us feel hopeless.

Name a few other things that lead to hopelessness: _____

_____

TODAY'S TREASURE
"O, Israel, put your hope in the LORD, for with the LORD is unfailing love and with him is full redemption."
Psalm 130:7, NIV

Loss can make us feel hopeless. So can a betrayal or a health diagnosis. Jeremiah 29:11 has been a stream in the desert for God's people for centuries. Relish the words in the Holman version: " 'For I know the plans I have for you'—this is the LORD's declaration—'plans for your welfare, not for disaster, to give you a future and a hope.' " Satan, the great counterfeiter, also knows the plans he has for you. Figuring out what they are is not difficult because they are the polar opposite of God's.

Let's try something to make a point. As if from the pen of Satan himself, write the absolute reverse of Jeremiah 29:11:

_____

_____

No matter what has happened, you are not hopeless. Satan's native language is deception. Christ Jesus defied the laws of nature to become the very embodiment of your hope and your future. As we soak both feet in the hope of Psalm 130 today, we will concentrate on verses 5-8.

Glance back over your previous lesson and read the HCSB translation of these verses. How would you describe the theme of the second half of Psalm 130?

_____

What did the psalmist picture as a comparison for a person waiting on the Lord?

○ a handmaiden   ○ a watchman   ○ a lion

Perched on a city wall, the ancient watchman served the original nightshift. He watched for nothing more closely than morning itself. The fate of the entire village rested on his shoulders. If he dozed or became distracted, enemy forces could overtake him. His eyes constantly searched the horizon for hints of anything unusual.

In some ways the watchman's ears were even more important to his task, enabling him to hear what he could not see. No more beautiful sight existed for the watchman than the sun raising its fiery head on the eastern horizon. The watchman could gather up his robes, store his weapons, kiss his wife good morning, and fall in the bed with the relief of a job accomplished. Some called him brave. After he'd spent the black of night scared of his own shadow and jumping at the sound of a breaking twig, he knew when morning came safely that he wasn't brave. He was *blessed.*

The psalmist described his posture as exceeding the one practiced by the city watchman. Fill in the following blanks according to verse 6.

"I wait for the LORD _____ than watchmen for the morning—

_____ than watchmen for the morning."

The psalmist wasn't watching for morning. He was watching for the one who owned the morning. His eyes were fastened to the horizon for a glimpse of God's presence. The Hebrew words translated "wait" (*qawah*) and "hope" (*yahal*) in Psalm 130 both include the indivisible element of expectation.[4] Likewise, the Greek term translated "hope" (*elpis*) loses all meaning without anxious expectation.[5]

Nothing is more critical than expectation to understand biblical hope and this psalm. Though the psalmist was convinced that his own poor decision had aggravated his plight, he placed his hope in what God's Word said about confession and forgiveness, he sought his God, and then he fully expected God to show up in his circumstances.

The psalmist petitioned God from up on his tiptoes in a posture ready to receive. Does that sound like how you usually approach God? ○ yes ○ no

By all means, if it does, say yes! But if you're more like me, when you feel like your own mistakes added insult to injury in your circumstances, you're more prone to hang your head in prayer than to lift it in full expectation of God's forgiveness and full redemption.

I'm about to get personal with you, but the vulnerability is worth it if it invites you to relate or helps make a point. Keith and I had a difficult marriage and desperately needed a miracle from God to make it. I had almost no confidence in my petitions before God's throne because I knew our hardships were direct results of a sinful relationship we'd shared before we were married. In fact, we were still so emotionally unhealthy that we had a long way to go toward sanctifying our sexuality. Satan, the accuser of all God's children, tried to convince me that Keith and I could expect little from God because we'd done so much wrong. "We should never have gotten married," I reasoned. Therefore, there was only so much that could be done.

Can anybody relate? Sexual sin is not the only place guilt can eclipse our expectation for God to act. Parents can feel like they blew it so badly with a child that his future—or their future relationship with him—is, at best, limited.

What is another example of how guilt can eclipse expectation?

We are often convinced that the more we can be blamed for our plight, the less God can do about it. What muddies the waters is that we're often right in the solely natural realm. Where do you think the adage "You made your bed, now sleep in it" comes from? A lawyer explains to his client that the plea bargain of 25 years in prison is the best they can do because of what he or she has done. What the prisoner may not factor in is God's ability to come within the confines of those very bars and set his captive soul freer than he has ever been.

When we cry out to God from the depths, taking full responsibility for our sins, our Champion *will* show up. If we put our hope in what His Word says is true, we can pray with absolute—if tearful—expectation that our God is coming. He will do more than save the day. He will save His child. We need not shrink back from God to soften His hard blows. God never comes to a truly repentant child with anger. He comes with unbridled affection. You see, we may have failed God but He will not fail us, "for with the LORD is unfailing love" (Ps. 130:7, NIV). Psalm 130:7 has become part of my life message and I'll likely share what it has come to mean to me as long as I live.

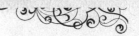

Glance back at Today's Treasure. What else is with the Lord besides unfailing love?

PRINCIPAL
QUESTION

To redeem something is to ransom it or buy it back if it originally belonged to you. The Hebrew *padhah* is certainly not limited to matters involving sin.[6] What you need redeemed most may have resulted from someone else's sin.

Psalm 130 tells us that our covenant God not only redeems but also He redeems in full. What does that mean to you today?

Keith's parents did not sign up for what they got in a daughter-in-law. They knew nothing about religious backgrounds like mine or vocations like mine. They'd never known a woman Bible teacher, and they certainly didn't expect to see their daughter-in-law on TV talking about things that their generation feels are better kept private. I've nearly scared them to death, but they have been patient, loving, and gradually accepting through the years.

I had the sweetest conversation with them a few days ago. The first copy of my book *Get Out of That Pit* had just rolled off the press and into my hands. I sat on the ottoman in their den and asked them if I could read the foreword their son had written for it. I knew it would sting because it made reference to the tragic and painful death of their firstborn. But the foreword was beautiful and I wanted them to see what God had done in the life of their secondborn.

I explained, "I don't know if you realize what God did when He brought Keith and me and the pain of our pasts together; but I believe with all my heart that, if you did, you would be so glad. Just think: Keith has a background of terrible loss through the death of a brother and later a sister. I have a background of child abuse. People out there can't think of anything worse than the death of a child and the abuse of a child. Yet together your son and I are proof that God can heal the worst of hurts and also use them to help other people." They both nodded lovingly and called us the next day to say they loved the foreword … and loved me.

Full redemption is what I described to my beloved in-laws who have loved me so lavishly without fully understanding me. Full redemption happens when God buys up or back everything that has happened to us and every sin we've committed.

Remember Jeremiah 29:11? Read it again; then consider the three verses that follow it carefully.

> " 'You will call to Me and come and pray to Me, and I will listen to you. You will seek Me and find Me when you search for Me with all your heart. I will be found by you'—the LORD's declaration—'and I will restore your fortunes and gather you from all the nations and places where I banished you'—the LORD's declaration. 'I will restore you to the place I deported you from.' " (HCSB)

PERSONAL QUESTION

What does the Lord declare He will restore, and how might the concept relate to you in spiritual terms?

Allowed to do so though our confession, invitation, and cooperation, God can restore our identity, our purity, our ability, and our sanity! He not only diffuses our past of all power to harm and haunt us but He *in*fuses it with power to help others. Redemption is incomplete if our negative past is only diffused. Satan won't be completely sorry and God won't get all the glory until the bad is used for good.

Did you stop too soon in the process, Beloved? Did you think God only wanted to diffuse your past? You may have stumbled onto the reason why you feel you can't get over it. The surrendered ground is not yet under your feet. Don't think you have to tell every detail of your personal past for God to use it. Your absolute authenticity and humility in ministry is often enough to turn the agony into glory.

As you conclude, put your own name in the blank and hear the voice of the Lord:

O _____, put your hope in the Me, the LORD, for with Me is unfailing love and with Me is full redemption.

Conclude your considerations of Psalm 130 by writing your own prayerful rendition. Then concisely express what God has said to you on your stair graphic. Thank you so much for the privilege of serving you today.

My Psalm 130

Things Too Great

A few moments ago I took a break and phoned Amanda to see how she and my grandson were doing. The way she whispered "hello" told me that our Little Bit, as I often call him, was taking a nap. Later we were both amused when we realized I was whispering too, as if he might hear me on the other end of the line.

Jackson has been fairly disinterested in his nap ever since he learned to pull up and stand in his crib. What a shame that we come to appreciate a good nap about the age we no longer have time to take one.

Amid dirty diapers in the pail and toys on the floor, Amanda had been in the Scriptures working on a devotional for our Web site. It reminds me that the lofty words of God were meant for the lowlands of planet Earth.

Our thoughts will be preoccupied today and tomorrow with one of the briefest yet loveliest Psalms of Ascent. David used the image of a child like our Little Bit to describe a great benefit in our relationship with God. While Psalm 131 is short on words, it is long on fodder for discussion. Go ahead and *say it*; then *work it*. At the end of day 4 perhaps we'll be ready with true authenticity to *pray it*.

TODAY'S TREASURE

"Lord, my heart is not proud; my eyes are not haughty. I do not get involved with things too great or too difficult for me."
Psalm 131:1, HCSB

PSALM 131 (HCSB)

A Davidic song of ascents.

1 LORD, my heart is not proud; my eyes are not haughty. I do not get involved with things too great or too difficult for me.

2 Instead, I have calmed and quieted myself like a little weaned child with its mother; I am like a little child.

3 Israel, put your hope in the LORD, both now and forever.

PSALM 131 (NCV)

1 LORD, my heart is not proud; I don't look down on others. I don't do great things, and I can't do miracles.

2 But I am calm and quiet, like a baby with its mother. I am at peace, like a baby with its mother.

3 People of Israel, put your hope in the Lord now and forever.

130

Like so many in the Gospels, the metaphors of the psalms came from common scenes and experiences in the daily lives of God's people.

- Psalm 126 pictured seeds watered by tears turning to sheaves of joy.
- Psalm 127 sketched sons, like arrows in a quiver, defending their father.
- Psalm 128 centered on the family table with moms like fruitful vines and children like olive shoots.
- Psalm 129 drew us the unforgettable picture of plowmen leaving furrows on the backs of the oppressed.
- Psalm 130 painted the image of a night watchman on a city wall.

God drew each metaphor from a common sight seen by a common people. Perhaps no sight was more ordinary than the one etched in Psalm 131, particularly as throngs of Israelites made their pilgrimage to Jerusalem three times a year. It's the same common sight I see every time I go shopping: a child in a mother's arms.

Psalm 131 reminds us the words of God are not primarily for seminaries, dissertations, and theological treatments. They are primarily for everyday living on the third rock from the sun. The words of God are for people who run late to work, hop out of the car, and spill coffee on their crisp, white shirt. It's for people who run to get their trash to the curb before the garbage truck comes and end up strewing it all over the driveway. It's for people who need to change the litter box and who realize something green and furry is growing in their fridge. The words of God are for people whose neighbors drive them nuts. And mainly, I suppose, for people who drive themselves nuts. Like me. Maybe like you.

If you've concluded that Scripture is for how you do church, teachers like me have failed you. Scripture is for how you do *life*, whether at home, at work or on a date, at a baby shower, at a funeral, or at church. Scripture is for servicemen defending their nation and for mothers nursing their babies … if they can keep their eyes open. Today we will be wholly preoccupied with the first verse of Psalm 131, and actually, we'll have to work diligently to limit ourselves to this space.

At second and third glance, you'll see that Psalm 131:1 bulges with potential discussion. But at first glance, what does Psalm 131:1 say to you?

PRINCIPAL QUESTION

_____

_____

_____

Most of us understand what the word proud *means. Offer a few synonyms for it:*

_____

The term *"haughty* comes from the word *high"*[7] and in the context of eyes it describes people who look down on others. Of course, none of us is going to immediately admit, "That's me!"

We recognize snobbery and pride pretty easily in others and despise nothing more. Somehow when we are the snob, however, the thin air at the altitude where we keep our noses impairs our judgment. The Bible tells us that God abhors pride and probably for no few reasons. Both you and I have had tug-of-wars with God—however ridiculous and futile—that revolved around our pride.

What are the top three reasons why you think God hates arrogance based primarily on the fruit of it in your own life?

_____

_____

_____

Since I made you answer such an exposing question, I'll offer a few reasons of my own. I am convinced that my pride over a specific matter was a tremendous contribution to the horrifying sifting season God put me through a few years ago.

I also think God cannot bring the kingdom increase to our harvests that He desires (John 15:7) until our egos decrease.

Finally, I think our pride is a strobe light flashing how ignorant we are about God, despite our lengthy quiet times and in-depth studies. Above all things besides love, humility is the truest sign of intimacy with God. Like little else, a humble spirit says we really do "get it."

Though Psalm 131:1 certainly applies to haughtiness and pride in general, when we consider the congregational aspect of the Psalms of Ascent, I think a tighter interpretation may be what we could call theological pride: arrogance regarding God, His words, or ways.

Stunning arrogance slithers down the halls of many academic institutions of theology. Thankfully, some professors are wise enough to slam their office doors and refuse to let the snake bite them, but they must be overtly intentional to resist a lure as old as the garden.

I wish the problem of theological snobbery only resided at institutions of higher learning, but it doesn't. Every one of us, until life pummels us into knowing better, is drawn to things that feed our flesh and make us feel smart.

Reflect on the words of Psalm 131:1 again: "I do not get involved with things too great or too difficult for me." I think this verse could very well refer to times when we get our big heads into matters we know nothing about—times we have the gall to speak for God or explain His actions when a wiser person would have kept her mouth shut. God has a fitting expression for it.

Humility is the truest sign of intimacy with God.

Read Job 38:1-2; then write verse 2 in your own words:

_____

_____

We've likely landed on the same kind of interpretation: "Who is muddying my counsel by talking about things he knows nothing about?" Ouch.

Now read Ecclesiastes 5:1-2. In most translations, verse 2 is comprised of two sentences. Write the second one in this space:

_____

_____

Obviously God is not saying that we are never to offer possible explanations for the deeper things of Scripture and its divine Author. Furthermore, we most assuredly need higher institutions of theology and well-trained professors. And a good debate between them can be tremendously insightful.

So, where's the line? How do we know when a matter is too great for us? Deuteronomy 29:29 may offer the best answer.

According to the verse, where you think the line of distinction, however faint at times, may fall?

_____

The things God has revealed are meant for us to study, ponder, teach, and share, though even then with discretion and wisdom regarding our hearer's capacity to handle them. The secret things, however, belong to God—for instance, exactly why planes hit buildings, tsunamis hit cities, and children get cancer.

Last year I stood with God-loving, Word-seeking friends at the Medical Center in Houston after their child and grandchild had been diagnosed with leukemia. The news came on the tail of several other tremendously difficult challenges God had entrusted to them. After all the things they'd already been through, all I could say with tears in my eyes was, "I don't know. I just don't know. I'm thrown too." A few days later Amanda called me sobbing and told me that a friend of hers from high school had been killed in a car accident along with her one-year-old baby. The most baffling part of all was the fact that several years ago, the parents of Amanda's friend had lost another adult daughter and her baby to a car accident. Follow me here: two children and two grandchildren lost to the same set of parents. What on earth?

I had no words for my daughter. In fact, I told her that I would have to get off the phone and call her back a little later. I hung up that phone and fell face down on the ground and cried so loudly that my next-door neighbors could have heard me. I beat the floor with my fists. I did everything but scream ugly words. But I couldn't get any words to come out of my mouth at all. I just kept crying, "Ohhhhh! Ohhhhh!"

The primary reason we are sometimes at a loss for words is that we *should be* at a loss for words. We're in over our heads and silence is our best option. And when the time for words does come, we're wisest to say what is true: "I just don't know why things like this happen, but I am so, so sorry." But later when no one else is around, how do we deal with these kinds of things within our own confused hearts?

PERSONAL QUESTION

Let me point the question straight to you: How do you deal with questions that seem to have no answers? If you deal with them poorly, say so. An honest appraisal is always best. If you've found a good way to deal with them, share it.

_____

_____

_____

_____

The way I personally get through confusing events like the ones I described is first to feel free to fall on the floor in the privacy of my own relationship with God and have a respectful fit. Second, when I get over the initial shock, I try to rehearse what I *do* know about God and His ways. Through the process, I am helped with what I *don't* know. Third, I often recall God's own description of Himself in Exodus 34:6-7 (HCSB): "Yahweh—Yahweh is a compassionate and gracious God, slow to anger and rich in faithful love and truth, maintaining faithful love to a thousand generations, forgiving wrongdoing, rebellion, and sin."

Over and over Scripture attests that God can do no wrong. It also blatantly assures us He is sovereign and could stop any ill. How can I make those ends meet? I can't … but God can and one day will. Between His arms that seem at times outstretched in opposite directions, you will find His heart. Out of the ashes of the unfathomable, sooner than later our Lazarus-faith must rise from the dead—questions still unanswered—or the Devil has won. Perhaps Anselm, an eleventh-century English monk, voiced an approach that draws today's lesson to the best conclusion:

> "I do not seek, O Lord, to penetrate thy depths. I by no means think my intellect equal to them: but I long to understand in some degree thy truth, which my heart believes and loves. For I do not seek to understand that I may believe, but I believe, that I may understand."[8]

Day Four

Like a Weaned Child

I'm so thankful God gave us one another. Sometimes when I'm writing to you God leads me to put some thoughts and difficult experiences on paper that I've not fully dealt with myself. I have sometimes worked out some things with God while I was working them on paper for you. God has used writing to invite me to hash some things out that otherwise I would have tried to put behind me prematurely. I hope you feel the same way as the study poses questions you otherwise might have avoided trying to answer. Surely at times you feel like I'm prying into your business. Actually God is prying into your business and mine.

Keith and I have a matching set of plain-looking black coffee mugs. When we fill them up with a hot drink, however, pictures of our grandson appear. Sometimes we are like those mugs. We don't know what will show up on us until God turns on the heat. His Spirit reveals feelings and long-held beliefs. The essence of wholeness is God winning us wholly with His affection, His truth, and His healing Word. Truly, God is our soul-ologist and pry He will, but never without loving intent.

Today is our second and final day to spend on the concise but rich words of Psalm 131. Please read the HCSB version again on page 130. On day 3 we talked about proud hearts and haughty eyes. Eugene Peterson's comments on our psalm bridge yesterday's lesson to today's:

> "But if we are not to be proud, clamorous, arrogant persons, what are we to be? Mousy, cringing, insecure ones? Well, not quite. Having realized the dangers of pride, the sin of thinking too much of ourselves, we are suddenly in danger of another mistake, thinking too little of ourselves. There are some who conclude that since the great Christian temptation is to try to be everything, the perfect Christian solution is to be nothing. And so we have the problem of the doormat Christian and the dishrag saint: the person upon whom everyone walks and wipes their feet, the person who is used by others to clean up the mess of everyday living and then is discarded. These people then compensate for their poor lives by weepily clinging to God, hoping to make up for the miseries of everyday life by dreaming of luxuries in heaven. Christian faith is not neurotic dependency but childlike trust. We do not have a God who forever indulges our whims but a God whom we trust with our destinies."[9]

Don't misunderstand. Scripture certainly tells us to cling to God whether we're weeping, wailing, or celebrating. Peterson was cautioning us against something he calls "neurotic dependency."

TODAY'S TREASURE

"Instead, I have calmed and quieted myself like a little weaned child with its mother; I am like a little child."
Psalm 131:2, HCSB

What do you think Peterson meant by "neurotic dependency"? _____

_____

We don't cure arrogance by becoming victims.

I think one thing he meant is that we don't cure arrogance by becoming victims. In a misguided attempt to be humble, we run the risk of not only becoming casualties of strong-willed people but of developing an even more toxic mind-set. We can come to see ourselves as God's victims, like rag dolls tossed about by His sovereignty and unrestrained power.

Offer a scenario depicting a way this could happen: _____

_____

The same psalm that teaches us not to occupy ourselves with questions too big for us also uses the metaphor of a content toddler resting on his mother to illustrate a quieted soul. God's goal is not children scared into silence but those who trust their parent even with questions unanswered. The quieted one in Psalm 131 has not been terrified into silence. We are not the victims of God but His cherished children.

Take the nearly inconceivable story of the parents who lost two children and two grandchildren in car accidents. That I could return to my Father's arms knowing He is in charge suggests either that: (1) I am like an abused dog who keeps returning to its cruel owner or (2) I know I can trust something about God's heart, come what may.

I am deeply touched that of all metaphors God chose the one of a weaned child with his mother. Probably every mother would be deeply moved that God drew a picture of a toddler resting in maternal love. God is not insecure about His masculinity; He is not reluctant to use the picture of a mother's love for her child as we try to imagine His care for us. He sketches the familiar image onto the family canvas and then says, "Now imagine something far beyond it." God often likens His care to a parent and sometimes as a mother to teach us that though He is but one parent, and He is Father, He is everything we need.

PRINCIPAL QUESTION

Please look up each of the following verses and note specific ways God parents:

Deuteronomy 1:31 _____

Deuteronomy 32:18 _____

Isaiah 46:3-4 _____

Isaiah 49:15 _____

Isaiah 66:13 _____

Which segment speaks most personally to you? Why?

_____

_____

_____

"I have calmed and quieted myself like a little weaned child with its mother; I am like a little child" (HCSB). You might wonder why the Scripture describes a weaned child rather than a nursing child … unless, of course, you've been around one recently. If you will allow me to have some wholesome fun with you about a wholesome womanly subject, a young mom said something once I've thought about hundreds of times since.

I was the first of my circle of friends to get married and pregnant, and I had few chances to be around others just ahead of me. I was barely showing when I met a friend of Keith's family who had a four-month-old daughter. I have always been baby crazy, so I had the infant in my arms in record time. A little while later, fearing that I'd imposed myself, I offered the baby to her mother. "Here. I bet you want her back." She said with the cutest expression "Are you kidding? Mama means dinner!"

I imagine many a nursing mom knows exactly what she meant. Before a baby is weaned, he or she often seems to think, _If Mom is going to hold me, she might as well make good use of herself and nurse me._ Nope, based on what I've seen, I wouldn't necessarily characterize an unweaned child as calm and quiet with his mother unless, of course, she's busy nursing.

According to the _Word Biblical Commentary,_ "Weaning from breast feeding took place around the age of three."[10] Honestly, can you picture a cuter age for a child in our metaphor—or a busier one?

Just this morning our 10-month-old grandson got one of his first bumps on the head from pulling up and then tumbling down. If he could, he'd move from one trouble spot to another, forsaking every toy for something more interesting … and dangerous. I laughed with Amanda and then said from experience, "You'll want to set him up for as many _yeses_ as you can because you're going to find that you will spend much of his next three years saying _no!_"

Jennifer Hamm, one of my staff members at Living Proof Ministries, told us a story a few days ago about her three-year-old son, Nathan, that still has us laughing. Jennifer and her family were leaving a restaurant with her friend Shannon and her family. On the way out, Shannon grabbed a few of the hard candies at the checkout counter and handed one each to the kids who are, by this time, old enough to handle them. Nathan loved the candy, chewed it up as quickly as he could, returned to his mom's friend and politely inquired, "Miss Shannon, may I please have another choking hazard?" Since that's what his mom had always called hard candies, he assumed "choking hazard" was their name.

Is anything a bigger handful than a three-year-old? When was the last time you tried taking every step one of them took? Weren't you exhausted? And yet when they've worn themselves out and the day is done, they've had their baths and squirmed into their jammies, hair still damp and smelling so good, they finally give up the fight and fall sound asleep … safe in their mommy's arms. Tomorrow there will be more battles to fight, but for now the child lets down his guard, lets his parent be in charge, and surrenders every care in the world.

The older I get, the more I like thinking of myself as God's child. Life gets so hard at times and the burdens so heavy, I occasionally feel 100 years old. You too? Not long ago as I put Melissa back on an airplane to grad school, she looked at me after I hugged her tightly and said, "Will I always be your baby?"

"Always, Darling. *Always.*"

And you, Dear One, will always be God's. "Like toddlers who soon run out of their own limited resources and gladly submit to being carried, we find God to be the One on whom we can depend to bring us to our destined goal, and one who already in Christ gives us rest for our souls."[11]

Write your own version of Psalm 131 and fill in your stair graphic. While you're at it, feel loved.

My Psalm 131

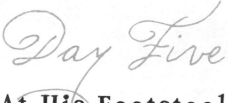

At His Footstool

Today we place the first foot on the thirteenth step in our ascent. You will soon discover that Psalm 132 is completely distinct among the Psalms of Ascent. Its most obvious difference is its length. Most of the songs are brief, well suiting them for memorization. Psalm 132 stands in stark contrast, measuring 18 verses. For this reason you'll find the first half of the psalm in today's lesson and the remainder in day 1 of week 6. To keep from overwhelming you at the end with the challenge to rewrite the entire psalm as your prayer, I have also included space at the end of today's lesson for you to pray the first portion only.

The tone and subject matter of Psalm 132 are also quite different. "This is the tenth of eleven *royal psalms* scattered throughout the book of Psalms."[12] Some scholars believe Solomon rather than David penned the inspired words because "this psalm was written as a prayer on behalf of King David"[13] and is referenced as early as the dedication of the temple in Solomon's reign (2 Chron. 6:41).

As different as Psalm 132 may seem from the other Psalms of Ascent, its subject matter makes perfect sense. Jerusalem was the destination city of Jewish pilgrims. This psalm recounts the history of how it became the central place of worship and God's presence. The natural break in Psalm 132 is in verse 11. Today's segment (vv. 1-10) is essentially David's oath to God and the petitions surrounding it. The next segment (vv. 11-18) is the record of God's response. Dive into the first portion of your thirteenth Psalm of Ascent, *say it, work it,* and then at the conclusion of today's lesson, *pray it.*

TODAY'S TREASURE
"Let us go to His dwelling place; let us worship at His footstool."
Psalm 132:7, HCSB

PSALM 132:1-10 (HCSB)

1 LORD, remember David and all the hardships he endured,
2 and how he swore an oath to the Lord, making a vow to the Mighty One of Jacob:
3 "I will not enter my house or get into my bed,
4 I will not allow my eyes to sleep or my eyelids to slumber
5 until I find a place for the LORD, a dwelling for the Mighty One of Jacob."

PSALM 132:1-10 (The Message)

1 O GOD, remember David, remember all his troubles!
2 And remember how he promised GOD, made a vow to the Strong God of Jacob,
3 "I'm not going home, and I'm not going to bed,
4 I'm not going to sleep, not even take time to rest,
5 Until I find a home for GOD, a house for the Strong God of Jacob."

6 We heard of the ark in Ephrathah;
    we found it in the fields of Jaar.
7 Let us go to His dwelling place;
    let us worship at His footstool.
8 Arise, LORD come to Your resting place,
    You and the ark that shows Your strength.
9 May Your priests be clothed with righteousness,
    and may Your godly people shout for joy.
10 Because of Your servant David,
    do not reject Your anointed one.

6 Remember how we got the news in Ephrathah,
    learned all about it at Jaar Meadows?
7 We shouted, "Let's go to the shrine dedication!
    Let's worship at God's own footstool!"
8 Up, GOD, enjoy your new place of quiet repose,
    you and your mighty covenant ark;
9 Get your priests all dressed up in justice; prompt
    your worshipers to sing this prayer:
10 "Honor your servant David; don't disdain your
    anointed one."

In one sentence, what does Psalm 132:1-10 recall? _____

_____

In a word, how would you describe King David's tone in these verses? _____

Psalm 132:1-10 recalls the fire in David's soul to have the ark of the covenant in the city of Jerusalem. Glance at Exodus 25:21-22. Why was the ark so significant?

_____

PRINCIPAL QUESTION

Associated with the Shekinah glory of God, the ark was the central location of worship in the Old Testament. What is it called in Psalm 132:7?

O *God's footstool*   O *God's throne*   O *God's altar*

The ark as God's footstool explained how God could be enthroned in absolute grandeur in an unseen kingdom yet still center some manifestation of His presence at a location on earth. The metaphor conveys Him seated on a throne in heaven (Isa. 6; Ezek. 1; Rev. 4) and propping His feet on earth by way of the ark of the covenant.

The history of the ark began following the exodus of God's people from Egypt. The Israelites built the ark and carried it according to sacred instructions through the wilderness on their 40-year trek to Canaan. After they crossed the Jordan and entered the promised land, the ark was placed in Shiloh (Josh. 18:1).

During the era of the judges, the ark was transported to Bethel (Judg. 20:26-27), but by the opening pages of 1 Samuel, it rested in Shiloh once again. There at Shiloh the unthinkable happened. After defeating the Israelites, the Philistines captured the ark. However, terrible misfortune befell the enemies of God as a result of their audacity, and they sent the ark back to the Israelites.

Read 1 Samuel 7:1. Where was the ark taken? _____

The ark stayed in this location throughout the rule of King David's predecessor, Saul. Never much of a stickler for obedience, Saul obviously did not prioritize the ark enough to inquire of God there (1 Chron. 13:3). In Psalm 132:6 the writer described the search for the ark. "Jaar is only a shortened form of Kiriath-Jearim," a name that means "city of forests."[14]

After conquering Jerusalem and establishing it as the capital of God's people, David rightly called for the ark to be brought to the city. No wonder God referred to him as a man after His own heart! David wanted God's presence more than he wanted his next breath. He was jealous for the glory and worship of God and for sacred things to find their sacred places.

I ask not to stir an ounce of condemnation but to open a door of invitation. Have you ever felt a David-like passion for God's presence? Once we begin to sense God's presence and favor frequently, nothing is worth risking it. Perhaps He's already developed a David-like passion in you to see Him reveal Himself. Maybe you know some of what David meant when he petitioned God to "arise and come."

> *"We heard of the ark in Ephrathah; we found it in the fields of Jaar."*
> Psalm 132:6

If you can relate on any level, please share where God has stirred passion in you for His presence, His glory, or His activity. Try to be specific.

_____

_____

PERSONAL QUESTION

David's motive for transporting the ark was both pure and right. His means, however, was tragically unscriptural. He made the grievous mistake of not pouring over the Scriptures for the proper handling and transport of earth's most sacred vessel.

Please read the account in 2 Samuel 6:1-11. What happened? _____

_____

Describe David's reaction in a few words: _____

_____

What on earth possessed David to transport the ark of the covenant on an ox cart? According to 1 Samuel 6:6, that's how the Philistines had transported it, yet interestingly the Philistines who put the ark on the cart did not lose their lives.

Do you see the significance? God expects His people to possess the scriptural knowledge and appropriate awe to approach rightly what is sacred. Can you imagine how David felt when sudden tragedy interrupted ecstasy? Second Samuel 6:8-9 tells us David was "angry" and "afraid." Our psalm may refer to this season in David's life.

Fill in the blank according to Psalm 132:1 in the HCSB translation:

"LORD, remember David and all the _____ he endured."

One scholar explains, "The *hardships*, here, are unlikely to mean the youthful trials of David; rather, the heart-searchings which he brought to his task; perhaps also his shock and distress at the death of Uzzah."[15]

Like David, most true worshipers of God will experience "hardships" at one time or another—though, hopefully, not on such a dramatic scale. David had a passion for God. He saw God as his safe refuge and the lover of his soul. Suddenly God didn't "behave" like David thought He should. God did something that seemed out of character. Even terrifying. Have you ever encountered something you believed God had either done or allowed that scared you or made you angry? You may recall that I mentioned a few scenarios on day 3 that left me speechless and upset.

Do you have an example of a time when God didn't "behave" like you expected Him to? If so, explain briefly and respectfully.

_____

_____

Even the recollections hurt, don't they? One reason is because many times the answers are no clearer today than they were then. Do you need some good news? Me too, and it's imperative to our psalm. Every pilgrim knew how David's "hardship" turned out.

Even if you've read the segment before, read and relish 2 Samuel 6:6-15. Why do you think David mustered the courage to send for the ark of the covenant again?

_____

Can you handle one last reading? We need to know why David's second try was successful. Please read 1 Chronicles 15:11-15. What did he do differently?

_____

Stay with me here, Beloved. Our historical lesson will become practical as we wrap up our thoughts. Though Uzziah's death shocked, angered, and frightened David, he wrestled for three months until he came to a conclusion I'll paraphrase in first person as one who has been there:

I can't explain what happened, Lord, as I've had this fearful reminder of Your inconceivable holiness and power. But this I know: I cannot live without Your presence. You are everything to me. You are worthy of my praise, Lord. Worth everything I have to do to adjust and alter my life to draw close to You. Giving up nearness to You is out of the question. Knowing You is what I live for. You are my love, my light, my salvation. I will do anything to make my way to You, and I will move anything that slows Your way to me. Teach me Your ways, O Lord. Clear the path. Arise, my God, and come to me.

Oh, the relief to pinpoint any obstacle and to remove it with repentance and obedience. No wonder David danced! Perhaps you've been afraid of God or angry at Him about something but, if you've known intimacy with Him in the past, you're also most likely miserable at this "safe" distance. Invite Him back with the fullness of His presence and remember the lesson of Obed-Edom. God cannot abide near you without blessing you. Call for Him. Somewhere in the heavenlies the music is playing, and it's time for you to dance again.

Use the space below to write your own version of what I suggested earlier may have been on the heart and mind of David after "hardship." If it's not as applicable to you, use the space to simply respond to God today with whatever is beating within your heart.

My Psalm 132:1-10

viewer guide

SESSION FIVE

My Hope Is in the Lord

As we continue our pilgrimage through the Psalms of Ascent, we will focus on one of the most vital elements of the journey: our fellow pilgrims. Today we're going to talk about how to be the best possible traveling partners.

Jeremiah 41:1-10 will set our stage today. The seventh month indicates with

near certainty that the 80 pilgrims were coming to Jerusalem for the Feast of

_____.

Because Ishmael was so sly in his wickedness, the following casualties resulted:

• _____ pilgrims were slaughtered.

• _____ paid heavy tribute to their enemy.

• _____ the remaining people in Mizpah were taken _____,

including the _____ _____.

We too face huge opposition as we journey toward Mount Zion to celebrate the ultimate Feast of Tabernacles with God.

How can we be effective fellow sojourners on the way?

1. _____ _____ concerning the Enemy's schemes.

Second Corinthians 2:10-11 tells us to _____ people "in the

sight of Christ … in order that Satan might not _____ us.

For we are not unaware of his schemes."

2. Read Hebrews 10:24-25. _____ one another.

3. Read 1 Peter 4:7-8. _____ each other _____.*

4. Fill in the following blanks according to Nehemiah 4:16-18. This segment

describes how the exiles who returned in pilgrimage to Jerusalem responded

to vicious opposition as they sought to rebuild the temple: "From that day on,

half of my men did the work, while the other half were equipped with spears,

_____, bows and _____. The officers posted themselves

behind all the people of Judah who were building the wall. Those who carried

materials did their work with _____ _____ and held

a _____ in the _____, and each of the builders

wore his _____ at his side as he worked."

If we don't want to be counted among countless Christian casualties in our

pilgrimage, we too have to learn to _____ _____ each other

instead of _____ each other.

*Excerpts are from Randy Frazee's *Making Room for Life* (Grand Rapids, MI: Zondervan, 2003) and John Ortberg's *Everybody's Normal 'Til You Get to Know Them* (Grand Rapids, MI: Zondervan, 2003).

Week Six
Blessings from Zion

Day One: God talks Back
Day Two: A United Family of Man
Day Three: A United Family of God
Day Four: Bless the Lord
Day Five: The Lord Bless You

Principal Questions

1. What was the condition of the royal Davidic covenant stated in Psalm 132:12?

2. Why does the distinction "family is ordinarily acquired rather than chosen" make family complicated?

3. What two locations are connected by the picture the psalmist painted?

4. What is the basic message of the final Psalm of Ascent?

5. Which three psalms has God used to speak most clearly to you?

Day One

God Talks Back

TODAY'S TREASURE

"There I will make a horn grow for David; I have prepared a lamp for My anointed one."
Psalm 132:17, HCSB

We launch our final week of study together with Scriptures brimming with joy and answered prayer. The second half of Psalm 132 stands as a wonderful reminder of why God is so worthy of our passionate pursuit—even in the aftermath of something frightening or maddening. Verses 1-10 are petitions to God in remembrance of His beloved King David and today's segment is God's astonishing response.

We get to begin today with the most obvious element of Psalm 132. Never lose sight of its wonder: *God answers us when we talk to Him.* Our thirteenth Psalm of Ascent displays a dialogue between God and man. A human spoke and the Divine responded. Please say it, work it, and at the conclusion of the lesson, pray it.

PSALM 132:11-18 (HCSB)

11 The LORD swore an oath to David, a promise He will not abandon: "I will set one of your descendants on your throne.

12 If your sons keep My covenant and My decrees that I will teach them, their sons will also sit on your throne, forever."

13 For the LORD has chosen Zion; He has desired it for His home:

14 "This is My resting place forever; I will make My home here because I have desired it.

15 I will abundantly bless its food; I will satisfy its needy with bread.

16 I will clothe its priests with salvation, and its godly people will shout for joy.

17 There I will make a horn grow for David; I have prepared a lamp for My anointed one.

18 I will clothe his enemies with shame, but the crown he wears will be glorious."

PSALM 132:11-18 *(The Message)*

11 GOD gave David his word, he won't back out on this promise: "One of your sons I will set on your throne;

12 If your sons stay true to my Covenant and learn to live the way I teach them, Their sons will continue the line— always a son to sit on your throne.

13 Yes—I, GOD, chose Zion, the place I wanted for my shrine;

14 This will always be my home; this is what I want, and I'm here for good.

15 I'll shower blessings on the pilgrims who come here, and give supper to those who arrive hungry;

16 I'll dress my priests in salvation clothes; the holy people will sing their hearts out!

17 Oh, I'll make the place radiant for David! I'll fill it with light for my anointed!

18 I'll dress his enemies in dirty rags, but I'll make his crown sparkle with splendor. "

If we could hear the voice of God as we sit before Him, we would never cease praying. If we realized how much the sovereign Creator esteems our passion and leans forward to hear our vows to Him, our relentless search for significance would finally end. God not only speaks in words not openly obvious, but He also responds to many of the things we say to Him through our Bibles. Because the words are not audible, we don't realize that God is often engaging with us in dialogue.

On a scale of 1 to 10, how convinced are you that your prayer time is an honest-to-goodness two-way communication? (1=not at all, 10=thoroughly)

1	2	3	4	5	6	7	8	9	10

One of the most spectacular elements of Psalm 132 is how God's answers exceeded the psalmist's petition. God appears to thoroughly enjoy doing "immeasurably more than all we ask or imagine" (Eph. 3:20, NIV) and probably has few bigger frustrations than when our prayerlessness denies Him the chance. You see, if we don't "ask or imagine," what does God have to out-do?

Glance at the first half of the psalm on pages 139-140 and compare it with today's segment of Scripture. Note any ways God's response went beyond the psalmist's pleas.

_____

_____

Our finite minds simply cannot grasp God's infinite ways of answering prayer.

God has done the same for you, Beloved, and here's the amazing part: He's answered you above and beyond what you asked on some of the very requests you assumed He answered negatively. If time and opportunity have passed, we assume God said no. Sometimes we're right. Sometimes we're wrong. Our finite minds simply cannot grasp God's infinite ways of answering prayer. You have no idea how many times you've prayed and God answered affirmatively but is awaiting the proper time for its revelation. Somewhat like Matthew 16:19, the answer has been "loosed" in heaven but hasn't yet been "loosed" on the pavement of earth. When the revelation does come, we sometimes don't link it with what we originally asked because we don't recognize the super-sized Ephesians 3:20 answer.

The scenario I just described is exactly what happened in Psalm 132. On what condition, stated in verse 12, did the royal Davidic covenant depend?

PRINCIPAL QUESTION

The "sons" of David and the kings who followed did not keep the covenant of obedience to God. Over and over they fell into idolatry until God did exactly what He promised. He allowed both the Northern Kingdom (*Israel*) and the Southern Kingdom (*Judah*) to fall into captivity. However, God in His great mercy kept His part of the covenant despite what His people deserved.

I love the way one commentator describes the transition playing on the concept of the psalms as songs: "the royal psalms survived, and the promises they contained were transposed into a new key. What were originally descriptions of the ruling king were pushed into the future and, taken together, provided a portrait of a great future king, a messiah (anointed one), who would come from the line of David."[1]

Hot diggity-dog!

I feel like responding with something really scholarly and mature like, "Hot diggity-dog!" I love nothing better than an Old Testament reference to Jesus Christ, our King. Another commentator adds, "This heightened fulfillment points beyond the present to the future messianic age, which is how the rabbis understood this closing section of the psalm prior to the Christian era. Many Old Testament prophetic passages were understood to be about the messiah until the claims of Christians that they had been fulfilled by Jesus caused the rabbis to view them differently."[2]

Reread Psalm 132:12,17-18 in the HCSB. Then look up each of the following references and draw a line matching them to their specific descriptions concerning the one God promised as a fulfillment of His covenant.

A forever throne	Revelation 11:15
A horn	Revelation 21:22-23
A lamp	Luke 1:68-69
My anointed one	Revelation 19:12
A glorious crown	Matthew 16:15-16

The Matthew reference is last so that you would only have one choice remaining since the link is veiled. The name *Christ* or *Messiah* means "the anointed one." Psalm 132 has a few other significant links to Christ that require explanation to recognize. The first is only a possibility to stir our imagination. Remember Psalm 132:6? It reads, "We heard of the ark in Ephrathah; we found it in the fields of Jaar."

We identified *Jaar*. Ephrathah is "the name either of Bethlehem itself or of a district in which Bethlehem was located."[3] Micah 5:2 foretells the birthplace of Christ: "Bethlehem Ephrathah, you are small among the clans of Judah; One will come from you to be ruler over Israel for Me. His origin is from antiquity, from eternity." In Luke 2:15 the shepherds heard from a great company of angels that the Christ child had been born in this very location. Far exceeding the ark, the body of Jesus was the sacred vessel, the One and Only "Word made flesh" where God revealed His utmost glory.

Let's meditate on one last messianic link in Psalm 132. As you'll soon see, the psalm makes priestly references to this coming king, yet the roles never mixed in Judaism. Kings and priests had completely separate roles and responsibilities. If a king presumed to take on a priestly duty, he could meet a severe judgment of God. In the order of the mysterious "Melchizedek," only the Messiah will fulfill both roles.

Psalm 132 intimates this priest-king in the prophesied fulfillment of the Davidic covenant. In his commentary on the Psalms, Kidner explains that, in Psalm 132:18, "the word used for *crown*" is "the same as for the high priest's mitre."[4] The priest's mitre represented his absolute sanctification, bearing the inscription upon his forehead, "HOLY TO THE LORD" (Ex. 28:36, HCSB).

Follow me one step further. The HCSB tells us in Psalm 132:18 that "the crown he wears will be glorious." A literal translation of the word "glorious" is "will blossom" and is "perhaps a reminder, too, of the rod whose blossom was God's accrediting of His high priest Aaron."[5] Christ's crown will be the glorious culmination of royalty and priesthood. As joint heirs of Christ and members of His royal priesthood, we ourselves are reflected in the praise of Revelation 1:5-6.

Read below Revelation 1:5-6. Circle what Christ "has made us."

"To Him who loved us and washed us from our sins in His own blood, and has made us kings and priests to His God and Father, to Him *be* glory and dominion forever and ever. Amen" (Rev. 1:5-6, NKJV).

Beloved, what kind of impact do these fulfillments have on you personally?

PERSONAL QUESTION

Reflect on the words of Psalm 132:16 from The Message as we close: "I'll dress my priests in salvation clothes; the holy people will sing their hearts out!" Those of us who know Jesus personally are among those very priests dressed in salvation clothes. Christ Jesus is the "yes" and "amen" (2 Cor. 1:20) to every promise of God in Psalm 132. As the ancient people of God made their arduous journeys to Jerusalem after sin and exile, they sang this song with hearts in their throats, fearing their disobedience had deferred their hope forever. Then when they least expected it,

"Joseph also went up from the town of Nazareth in Galilee, to Judea, to the city of David, which is called Bethlehem, because he was of the house and family line of David, to be registered along with Mary, who was engaged to him and was pregnant. While they were there, the time came for her to give birth. Then she gave birth to her firstborn Son, and she wrapped Him snugly in cloth and laid Him in a feeding trough—because there was no room for them at the inn. In the same region, shepherds were staying out in the fields and keeping watch at night over their flock. Then an angel of the Lord stood before them, and the glory of the Lord shone around them, and they were terrified. But the angel said to them, "Don't be afraid, for look, I proclaim to you good news of great joy that will be for all the people: today a Savior, who is Messiah the Lord, was born for you in the city of David" (Luke 2:4-11).

Pilgrim, sing your heart out! Your King has come.

Rewrite the last half of Psalm 132 into a prayer and fill in your stair graphic.

My Psalm 132:11-18

Day Two

A United Family of Man

Depending on the current emotional climate of your nuclear and extended family, today you will put what may be a road-weary foot on the fourteenth Psalm of Ascent. Psalm 133, comprised of three short verses, dwarfs in the shadow of the lengthy and stately Psalm 132 that has occupied our attentions for the last two days. Let's drag our next psalm out of that shadow and let it stretch its legs, however, because it has much-needed words to say to us.

Interestingly, the psalm will also offer us the opportunity to say some much-needed things in response—perhaps things you and I need to get off our chests. I expect this psalm and the discussions it invites will touch a nerve in you as it has in me … unless you live in virtual solitary confinement—and I pray for your sake and for others' that you don't. Let's jump in and apply the first two approaches to our fourteenth psalm: *Say it* and *work it*.

TODAY'S TREASURE
"How good and pleasant it is when brothers can live together!"
Psalm 133:1, HCSB

PSALM 133 (HCSB)

Living in Harmony
A Davidic song of ascents.
1 How good and pleasant it is
when brothers can live together!
2 It is like fine oil on the head,
running down on the beard,
running down Aaron's beard,
on his robes.
3 It is like the dew of Hermon falling
on the mountains of Zion. For there the LORD
has appointed the blessing—
life forevermore.

PSALM 133 (NLT)

A song for the ascent to Jerusalem. A psalm of David.
1 How wonderful it is, how pleasant, when brothers live
together in harmony!
2 For harmony is as precious as the fragrant anointing
oil that was poured over Aaron's head, that ran down
his beard and onto the border of his robe.
3 Harmony is as refreshing as the dew from Mount
Hermon that falls on the mountains of Zion. And
the LORD has pronounced his blessing, even life
forevermore.

I have a theory about what prompted Psalm 133 to become part of this liturgy. The psalm celebrates unity. I think we don't truly appreciate unity without *unappreciating* disunity. We don't appreciate how "good and pleasant it is" when family members live together in unity until we've encountered how negative and unpleasant it is when they don't. The Message reads, "How wonderful, how beautiful, when brothers and sisters get along!" Did those words get a strong affirmation from you? Perhaps because you've encountered the opposite? As we draw our journey to conclusion, never forget that the psalms are for real people—not robots. They're for humans with all manner of personality flaws and unmet emotional needs. Don't you think dads got grumpy with their kids then just as now? Don't you think women still got PMS? Ancient people were no less human. They annoyed one another just like we do.

Hence, my theory: I think they joyfully anticipated the gatherings, but the reality of the trip could beg another perspective. I suspect they looked forward to being with Uncle Hosea, cousin Jedediah, and Gran-Bethlebigma, but they probably forgot how annoying some of their personal habits were until they got on the road together. They'd forgotten how much Uncle Hosea spits. And how cousin Jedediah eats with his mouth open. And how Gran-Bethlebigma takes her teeth out after dinner. (Why can't she wait until bedtime?) Traveling long distances only exaggerated the challenges.

Think back on times you've taken long trips with people, family or not. Based on those experiences, what makes traveling together particularly challenging?

Think of someone with whom you enjoy traveling. What makes it work?

Only one thing is trickier than being in close quarters with family: *traveling in close quarters with family*. Psalm 133 extols the virtues of family unity, not because it came easily but because when it came it was delightful.

I didn't derive my theory from depth of insight. I got it from the Christmas holidays. Our home happily teemed with nuclear and extended family company for two weeks. At various times four generations graced our brick and mortar. Cousins' voices raised the roof. I put the last visiting family member on an airplane only two days ago. We had a blast! We made memories that we'll take to our graves. (Or will ultimately put us there.) We hugged, kissed, and sat on one another playfully. But we also had a few fireworks and a few less obvious smoldering embers.

You see, Beloved, I have a real, live family. We don't live in Stepford. We live in Realville. We still have some fights and hurt feelings at our house. The Moore/Jones/Green extended family loves passionately and can tangle passionately. The day I acquire the perfect family I won't be of much use to you. I don't know about you, but I don't need a pastor or a Bible study teacher who has it all together. That person will cease having anything to say to me. God's Word is meant for real families and real

God's Word is meant for real families and real problems.

problems and those are the kinds of applications this sojourner needs. Since I don't see any signs of the perfect family on the Moore horizon, I reckon I'll hang in here and attempt to serve you a little longer.

How about you? Any signs of the perfect family? ○ yes ○ no

Without specifying names, what are a few of the most challenging imperfections within your nuclear and/or extended family?

Today we will apply the psalm to our physical families or what I called in the day's title *the family of man.* Tomorrow we're going to apply it to *the family of God* as we follow the transition of Psalm 133 from a smaller to broader scope. For the remainder of our lesson, let's consider one dimension that makes the unity ascribed in today's psalm so complicated: *family is ordinarily acquired rather than chosen.*

Why does not necessarily having chosen relationships make family complicated?

PRINCIPAL QUESTION

We didn't get a say in most of those who share our homes and family reunions. We may choose our college roommates, but we acquired most of our kin. Perhaps we've all heard the saying, "Friends are family you got to choose." The difference is real.

We form most friendships out of personal preferences, but we're not automatically the better for it. (Stay with me here. This lesson may bruise my feet more than yours.) Many of us have distanced ourselves from extended family because we've replaced them with people we prefer. Though some elements of the transition are justified and godly, others are selfish. Let's face it. Family is more trouble than friendship, and the fear that we might share similarities with some of our members also carries an indictment too strong to face on a regular basis.

For one thing, we can drop friends more easily when the relationship becomes inconvenient. Here's the rub and maybe the help: God chose our family even if we didn't. Even the challenges they pose can be effective motivation to seek His throne, His help, and His healing (AKA: deal with our stuff.) After all, where would our prayer lives be without family? Furthermore, if we only choose to be around those who require virtually nothing hard from us, what will prompt us (force us) to change?

Think of someone in your life God has most used to make you seek change. Without mentioning his or her name, what about the person made you need to change?

PERSONAL QUESTION

I love serving single women as much as married women. If you are single and living alone, however, I want to love you enough to point out the risk of avoiding needed change. People who live in close quarters with others have someone constantly trying to knock off their rough edges. People who live in community can also learn a little more readily that a fight need not be a fatality. They can learn a bit more easily how to apologize because they are invited to do it. On the other hand, someone living alone could manage most of the inconveniences and difficult personalities right out of their personal lives. He or she might rewrite Psalm 133:1 to say, "How good and pleasant it is when kindred live somewhere else." Pleasant? Maybe. Good? Not necessarily. God often uses other people as the chisel to carve true integrity into our rough personalities. A chisel that never scrapes the stone is useless.

Don't misunderstand me to say you shouldn't live alone. If I were single, I'd probably want to too. Just make sure you stay closely connected with a family-like group of people to be blessed, coaxed, irritated, and motivated enough by them to keep changing. Learning to endure hardship and inconvenience with people is critical to the process of becoming a whole person. When all is said and done, some of the people we needed most to fulfill God's plan for our personal lives will be those we wanted least. God doesn't just want us to be happy; He wants us to be useful.

How have you discovered this to be true? _____

_____

Earlier I suggested that we may not have chosen our family members, but God did. That doesn't mean God chooses all their actions and decisions. God does not tempt people to sin. He does at times, however, permit difficult things to happen within families. To paraphrase Joseph's words to his brothers in Genesis 50:20, what Satan and others mean for evil in our lives, God wouldn't have allowed unless it could be used for good and for the delivering of lives.

As we conclude, meditate on the following quote out of the New Interpreter's Bible commentary: "The family is a crucial institution. It affects everyone, for good or ill. By its very nature, it can be the place where one experiences and learns intimacy, love, and growth, or it can be the place where one experiences and learns resentment, abuse, and destructive behavior."[6]

Most likely the home in which you grew up was a mixed bag of love and hurt just like mine. Whatever happened to us didn't get to kill us as the enemy probably hoped. And if we're willing, it may be used of God to actually heal us. You and I are still alive and kicking and (Lord help us!) still changing if we're willing.

Family unity is not automatic. It's democratic. It takes a majority of people in a home casting their votes toward getting along. Lest you give up, keep in mind that every majority begins with one contagious person.

Filled with Christ's Spirit, that one person can be you.

A United Family of God

Today we place both feet on the fourteenth step in our ascent to the next level with God. We will transition from yesterday's focus on the *family of man* to the far broader *family of God*.

Please glance back at your previous lesson and reread Psalm 133. What two metaphors did the psalmist employ as expressions of kindred living together in unity?

First metaphor (v. 2): _____

Second metaphor (v. 3): _____

Students of Psalm 133 can well justify identifying the reference of "brothers living together" in verse 1 as close kindred. In the next two verses, however, the psalmist widened the range to include the entire people of Israel. We can draw that conclusion based on the metaphors you just noted. The reference to Aaron recollects a monumental moment in the history of Israel.

Read Exodus 29:1-9 and describe it briefly here: _____

_____

Glance back at Psalm 133:2. As a result of the division after Solomon's reign, some of the kingdom references in the historical annals of Israel could apply to the Northern Kingdom (Israel) or to the Southern Kingdom (Judah). *The priesthood, however, was all-encompassing.* It was established in the infancy of Israel and was dictated by God to be a lasting ordinance.

In Psalm 133 the portrait of unity painted by the anointing of Aaron was not lost on an Israelite. Following the exile and the destruction of the temple, pilgrims who returned to Jerusalem for the feasts surely did so with the fear that God may have removed His love from them and closed His ears to their petitions. To sing a song reminding them of their immutable anointing as the children of God was profound and no doubt emotional.

The second metaphor is equally rich. A moment ago I pointed out that references in Scripture to the priesthood were all-encompassing while references to the kingdom could apply to the Northern tribes *or* Southern tribes.

TODAY'S TREASURE
"It is like the dew of Hermon falling on the mountains of Zion. For there the LORD has appointed the blessing—life forevermore."
Psalm 133:3, HCSB

PRINCIPAL QUESTION

Read verse 3 carefully. Which two locations does the picture connect?

Zion   Hermon   Jerusalem   Bethlehem   Sinai

While we don't quickly catch the significance of connecting Mount Hermon to Mount Zion, Israelites who knew their history and geography certainly would. Mount Hermon, located strategically in the north, is the highest mountain in Israel. Its "summit reaches to about 9,100 feet, and receives more than 60 inches of annual precipitation,"[7] a fact that helps explain the reference in Psalm 133 to its dew. One commentator suggested that Mount Hermon's dew is so profuse that a person camping close to its peak would awaken to a tent fully saturated with the equivalent of a heavy rain.[8] In contrast, Mount Zion (Jerusalem) is located much farther south.

The idea of Hermon's dew falling on Mount Zion may have found great significance among the pilgrim songs because it gave imagery to "the people of the northern kingdom" flowing "down upon Zion, the center of the southern kingdom."[9] During those three pilgrim journeys a year, the wayward, broken streams of north and south came together as one river. "Behold, how good and how pleasant it is for brethren to dwell together in unity!" (KJV).

The tragic division into two kingdoms also resulted in loss of identity. The reason the people ultimately took on the name "Judah-ites" (shortened to "Jews") is because the tribe of Judah alone retained a measure of its unity. We may shake our heads and think *what a pity* before the reality hits us that Christians split into much more than half. We have splintered into every conceivable twisted branch of one family tree.

I'm not just referring to the denominations. I'm talking about divisive, unloving, and arrogant attitudes rising up from among those distinctions between blood-bought, grace-taught siblings. Eugene Peterson points out, "The first story in the Bible about brothers living together is the story of Cain and Abel. And it is a murder story. Significantly, their fight was a religious fight, a quarrel over which of them God loved best."[10] We're like that sometimes, aren't we? At the heart of our interfaith debates is our attempt to prove that God loves us—approves of us—more than our sibling. But our hearts toward one another can change. And we have the will of Christ to preapprove our request.

According to commentator John Eaton, the original wording in Psalm 133:1 literally translates, "the dwelling of brothers together as one."[11] Circle the word "one."

Read John 17:20-21, the rich words of intercession Christ prayed to His Father on the eve of the crucifixion. Answer the following questions based on those verses:

Who was the prayer for? _____

What was the prayer for? _____

Why did Christ want it? _____

I hope you participated in video session 5 as we talked about traveling partners in our journey to the heavenly Mount Zion. We talked about loving and respecting one another and serving next to one another "shoulder to shoulder," so tightly knit that no opposition could come between us (see Zeph. 3:9, NIV).

Instead of criticizing and mocking one another, we want to "be concerned about one another in order to promote love and good works, not staying away from our meetings, as some habitually do, but encouraging each other, and all the more as you see the day drawing near" (Heb. 10:24-25, HCSB). As I've shared before, I was greatly relieved and freed when God helped me understand that unity does not equal uniformity. In both the family of man and the family of God, we can be very different and yet still practice unity. We can get along and come to love each other even if, in our human nature, we wouldn't have preferred one another. I'm not sure many things are more fulfilling in the Christian experiences than, in the power of the Holy Spirit, finally having victory over an old area of religious prejudice.

We can be very different and yet still practice unity.

Have you experienced overcoming religious prejudice? If so, describe it briefly.

_____

Nothing is like the holy nod of God: the sense that He is pleased by our courage to go against the grain of prevailing opinions and our own putrid flesh in order to "let this mind be in" us that "was also in Christ Jesus" (Phil. 2:5, KJV).

Christ wants believers to be one: black, brown, or white. Charismatic or noncharismatic. Calvinist or Arminian. Southern Baptist or Freewill Baptist. Add a few more …

_____

What do we do about all our very real differences? I am a visual learner and some years ago as I first grappled with a strong burden toward unity in the body, God illustrated a concept to me through a diagram of a skeleton. I believe He showed me that among believers in the body of Christ there are spine issues of great importance and rib issues of less importance.

Spine issues comprise the backbone of our faith. They are biblical tenets of such importance that disagreement may mean one of us is in Christ and the other is not. Or they mean that one is highly deceived and the other is walking in Truth. Rib issues, in contrast, do not involve matters that threaten to break the back. Some of them may be important to us, but they are not matters of eternal life and death. Differences in rib issues tend to be more interpretive and less heretical. I've shared the concept of spine issues vs. rib issues a number of times, but I've never asked students to label a diagram for themselves. I'm so glad God caused me to wait until today as we camp on Psalm 133.

Based on the descriptions I gave you just a moment ago, meditate on several possible spine issues and rib issues; then label them on this diagram.

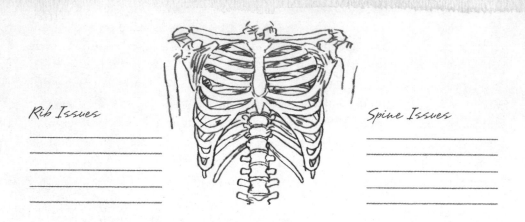

Rib Issues

_____
_____
_____
_____
_____

Spine Issues

_____
_____
_____
_____
_____

If you're participating in a small group, I'd love for you to talk about these in your gathering this week. But if you end up in debates, arguments, or offenses, the point will be lost! The goal is to realize that we don't have to agree on rib issues. We can still thoroughly love one another even if we remain mystified as to how the other grew that odd rib. Questions arising from our differences can also cause us to run to God's Word and see if what we believe is biblically sound.

I have rarely seen a person change her mind about a doctrinal stand because someone shouted at her about how wrong she was. On the other hand, I have seen countless people change their positions because something drove them to the Word of God. I saw one of them in the mirror this morning.

OK, I'll throw out a few of my spine issues: Jesus is the only way, truth, and life, and no one gets to God any other way. It's not popular, but it's the truth. (See John 14:6.) Furthermore, Jesus Christ came wrapped in human flesh as the divine Son of God. Nonnegotiable in my opinion. (See John 1:1,14; Col. 1:19-20.) I also believe Christ's bodily resurrection is an absolute tenet of the Christian faith. Christ's resurrection occurred as the firstfruit of the harvest so that all who believed in Him thereafter could be raised from the dead (see 1 Cor. 15:22-23). What about rib issues? Spiritual gifts, stands on the end times, and styles of worship. I wish I could see your diagram because I know we could have fun discussing it.

Take the "unity" out of "community" and what you have left doesn't even make sense. No one in the last century has contributed more to the concept of Christian community than German theologian Dietrich Bonhoeffer. At great expense, he led a "fugitive community of seminarians"[12] in the pursuit of truth during the Nazi regime. During that harrowing period, he penned the following words:

"Not what a man is in himself as a Christian, his spirituality and piety, constitutes the basis of our community. What determines our brotherhood is what that man is by reason of Christ. Our community with one another consists solely in what Christ has done to both of us."[13]

As we reflect on such powerful words of a man who lost his life for truth, let's each think of someone we tend to dislike and feel divisive toward in the body of Christ. Picture his or her face. Recall some of the things that cause you to feel so resistant.

Without writing a name, list several things he or she is "by reason of Christ":

Ask Christ to cause you to couple every thought you have about this person with these truths. Our first real steps toward unity are not toward those we naturally like. They're toward those we don't. Jesus' kind of unity doesn't exist until two people stand shoulder to shoulder who before stood sword to sword. Let's do the hard thing. Let's love each other when we wouldn't even like each other. After all, eternity is a mighty long time to spend together.

Surely "life forevermore" constitutes the perfect ending to a psalm applauding unity! Seen in its context, the psalmist implied that siblings dwelling together in unity comprise one of the great pleasures of life evermore. Just think about it. Every time brothers and sisters in Christ study together, worship together, eat together, or laugh our heads off together, amid all our distinctions, we really do get a small taste of heaven. And Christ gets a small taste of His own medicine. Behold, how good and pleasant it is!

Conclude by rewriting Psalm 133 in your own words and into a prayer; then fill in your stair graphic. I'm crazy about you.

My Psalm 133

Day Four
Bless the Lord

A little while ago I finished my research for our final Psalm of Ascent and placed 14 commentaries back on the shelf in my office. They'd been in a big box for months so that I could cart them from my office to my home on beautiful days when the back porch was perfect for writing. I sighed with a familiar sadness in my soul to see another journey come to an end. I dearly love being in the throes of an in-depth Bible study. Don't you? Don't you love digging up something in God's Word you've never discovered before? Or being reminded of something you'd forgotten? Don't you love having your mind challenged and your heart changed? And more than anything in this world, don't you love knowing Christ a little more fully than you did? Life doesn't get any better.

To me, the Amplified Version of Philippians 3:10 beautifully expresses each life's ultimate pursuit: "For my determined purpose is that I may know Him, that I may progressively become more deeply and intimately acquainted with Him, perceiving and recognizing and understanding the wonders of His Person more strongly and more clearly." With your face set like flint toward life's loftiest goal, please look to Psalm 134—your final step in this journey's ascent—and *say it, work it,* and prepare to *pray it.*

TODAY'S TREASURE
"Now praise the LORD, all you servants of the LORD who stand in the LORD's house at night!"
Psalm 134:1, HCSB

PSALM 134 (HCSB)

A song of ascents.

1 Now praise the LORD, all you servants of the LORD who stand in the Lord's house at night!
2 Lift up your hands in the holy place, and praise the Lord!
3 May the LORD, Maker of heaven and earth, bless you from Zion.

PSALM 134 (WBC)

Come, bless YAHWEH, all you servants of YAHWEH, who are standing in YAHWEH's house by night.
Raise your hands toward the holy place and bless YAHWEH
May YAHWEH bless you from Zion, the one who made heaven and earth.

What a wonderfully fitting end! The 15 pilgrim songs began in Psalm 120, far away from Jerusalem in the alien lands of Meshech and Kedar. The woe of surroundings they'd known "too long" (Ps. 120:6, HCSB) had not demoralized them as their enemy surely hoped. Instead, it heightened their anticipation for each arduous journey to Mount Zion and deepened their conviction not to miss it for the world.

Oh, that we would have such determined purpose! Psalm 121 followed with the pilgrims on their risky way. Mountains loomed, but a Watcher guarded them from the heavens. They recited their trust in God to be their help, to keep their feet from slipping, and to stay awake while they fitfully slumbered amid the harsh elements. Psalm 122 followed with words expressing the near ecstasy of arrival: "Our feet are standing in your gates, O Jerusalem" (v. 2, NIV)!

Psalms 123–133 filled the psalmists' mouths with a host of praises, themes, and petitions centered on everyday experiences such as farming and family. The choruses spoke of pain, repentance, redemption, and humility and coaxed their impatient souls to wait like watchmen for the Lord. The sojourner's songbook then concluded with "the highest point of ascent in this collection."[14]

Glance back on the Word Biblical Commentary translation of Psalm 134 and write the basic message of the final Psalm of Ascent:

PRINCIPAL QUESTION

I chose the WBC translation because I knew we'd more likely notice the repetition of the less familiar Yahweh *than the expected title,* LORD. *How many times is the name used in the three short verses?*

The other repetitive term is "bless." Psalm 134 is a call to bless our covenant God and to be blessed by Him. We will consider the call to bless Him today and the call to be blessed by Him tomorrow in our final lesson.

Meditate on comments in the New Interpreter's Bible: "After Psalm 133 has celebrated the unity of the gathered people of God in Zion, Psalm 134 addresses the gathered congregation, inviting them to do what they had come to Jerusalem to do: praise the Lord."[15]

Peterson echoed the thought: "The sentence ['Come, bless Yahweh'] is an invitation; it is also a command. Having arrived at the place of worship, will we now sit around and tell stories about the trip? Having gotten to the big city, will we spend our time here as tourists, visiting the bazaars, window shopping and trading? Having gotten Jerusalem checked off our list of things to do, will we immediately begin looking for another challenge, another holy place to visit? Will the temple be a place to socialize, receive congratulations from others on our achievement, a place to share gossip and trade stories, a place to make business contacts that will improve our prospects back home? But that is not why you made the trip: bless God. You are here because God blessed you. Now you bless God."[16]

Briefly summarize Peterson's basic point in your own words:

_____

I wrote: "Do what you came to do!" Of course, God blesses our fellowship and our shared experiences; each of those have important places in our travels here on earth. You and I, however, were created to praise God; so let's spend priority time doing what we came to do. I felt a tang of conviction over my attentions during worship at my own church. I dearly love the people who sit in my same general section and, goodness knows, God wants me to! He desires for us to embrace and be happy to see one another; but when worship begins, God wants us to push the hold button on our fellowship with one another and give Him 100 percent of our attention. He wants us to do what we came to do! Anybody else a tad convicted?

Our seasons of in-depth study are used of God to mold us in a myriad of ways, but many of the journeys God allowed me to write have priority goals. For instance, hopefully those who take *Breaking Free* really will emerge from the pages with a remarkable new measure of freedom. Prayerfully, those who do *Believing God* will receive a fresh anointing of faith. God help us, may those who finish *When Godly People Do Ungodly Things* become well-armed against satanic seduction.

As we turn the last page of our study of the Psalms of Ascent, our ultimate goal will be accomplished if we've ascended to the next level in the worship of our God. To take the next step in authentic praise and worship is to take the next step in multiple areas of our lives. If we are truer worshipers today than six weeks ago, we are truer lovers. Truer servers. Truer seekers. Truer confessors. We've learned that psalmist-worship rises like incense to the throne of Zion with utmost honesty yet inward hope. And with face-down conviction inviting chin-up redemption.

God came the last six weeks to make psalmists of us. He has engraved in our minds that psalms are for real people with real problems. They're for people with real jobs or without them, for people with real relationships or a lack of them. I wonder what your last six weeks have entailed. I am thoroughly convinced that God times our thematic journeys into His Word to speak into the experiences He knows in advance we will have. Daily living is such a concoction of pain and pleasure.

PERSONAL QUESTION

Give this exercise some thought before you complete it: List some highs, lows, celebrations, and frustrations you've experienced over the course of our study of the Psalms of Ascent:

Highs _____

Lows _____

Celebrations _____

Frustrations _____

When you began this study, you had a picture in your mind of what a psalmist looks like. In biblical terms, perhaps you imagined him like a shepherd with a harp under one arm and a lamb under the other. In modern terms he probably looked like your worship leader. The truth is, a psalmist looks like you.

Glance back to the list you just compiled. A psalmist's life looks just like yours, and the psalmist's song is never more clearly heard in the portals of heaven than when he offers his praise as a sacrifice in the darkest of nights. Psalm 134:1 (HCSB) calls us to "Praise the LORD, all you servants of the LORD who stand in the LORD's house at night!" *The International Critical Commentary's* verse 2 says, "In the dark night lift up your hands to the sanctuary and bless Yahweh."[17]

Night services were often held in the temple courts in association with the feasts. We learned of one perfect example in session 4. "Later Jewish tradition associates nocturnal services with the Feast of Tabernacles, the ceremony of water libation associated with the autumn festival."[18] Remember how we pictured the lamplights of those small shelters pitched as far as eye could see on the hills surrounding Jerusalem? We may know about the nights of the feasts, but what about the nights of the soul?

Read Job 35:9-10 and describe the point you believe he was trying to make:

_____

_____

By all means, we want to "cry out under" our "load of oppression" and "plead for relief from the arm of the powerful" (NIV), but we also want to seek our God and Maker and ask Him to give us songs in our night.

Ask any songwriter of our time and he or she will tell you that the clearest and deepest words God grants the soul are often those that come in a dark season of life. One of the dearest treasures in your darkness will be the God-song He will give you if you'll receive it. To stand in the presence of the Lord when you'd rather go to bed and never get up, and to praise Him in the night when taunting voices tell you to curse Him—these things are nothing less than a battle cry of victory. How can we know? When King Jehoshaphat and God's people were nearly overcome by a vast army of joint forces, 2 Chronicles tells us what he did after he sought the Lord.

Read 2 Chronicles 20:21 and record the action. _____

_____

Now read verse 22. What did God do? _____

_____

Beloved, worship is all we've discussed, but it is also warfare. What is the very first word of the **Holman Christian Standard Bible's** *translation of Psalm 134:1?*

_____

Don't wait! Praise God the second you don't feel like it! The second you feel defeated! "Now!" Your tempter tempts you to praise God the least when you need to praise the most. A true psalmist praises his way to victory, knowing it will come because the praise itself renders the first blow to his enemy's brow. God's faithfulness then calls for man's gratefulness. Inherent in the call to "bless Yahweh" is the cry to thank Him. In Karl Barth's words, "*Charis* always demands the answer *eucharitia*. Grace and gratitude belong together like heaven and earth. Grace evokes gratitude like the voice an echo. Gratitude follows grace as thunder follows lightning."[19]

Has God lit up your sky with lightening that you've not yet answered with thunder? Can you think of anything recently that you got too busy to stop and really thank Him for? That happens to me too. Let's make a little thunder right here:

_____

_____

_____

_____

Worship has endless side effects in the life of the everyday psalmist. Among them, it exalts God to the highest place, thereby relieving the sojourner of the backbreaking burden of ego. It defeats our enemy. It answers grace with gratitude. And it ends in joy. "God is a personal reality to be enjoyed. We are so created and so redeemed that we are capable of enjoying him. All the movements of discipleship arrive at a place where joy is experienced. Every step of ascent toward God develops the capacity to enjoy. Not only is there, increasingly, more to be enjoyed, there is steadily the acquired ability to enjoy it. Best of all, we don't have to wait until we get to the end of the road before we enjoy what is at the end of the road."[20]

The destination of any trip sets the tone of travel. You and I are not on our way to a funeral like many of those who surround us. We who are in Christ are on our way to a wedding of such glorious and expensive proportions that we'll have to change our clothes from mortal to immortal just to survive the thrill. Yes, as the psalmist said, joy cometh in the morning (Ps. 30:5, KJV), but the very anticipation invites it into our night.

The Lord Bless You

As we place both feet on our final Psalm today, I want to tell you again how much your part in this journey means to me. I submerged myself in God's Word long before writing studies. Each study has emerged out of the overflow of what God taught me in our own relationship. But I wonder if I would have studied as hard if you had not been along. I wonder if I would have looked at a fourteenth commentary without being driven by responsible scholarship. How much more have we sought God, grappled with difficult Scripture, and surrendered in obedience to Christ because we cheered each other on? As the verse in Hebrews 10:24 commands, we've stirred each other up. I am deeply grateful.

On day 4 we focused on the call to bless the Lord. Today we close by focusing on the reverse: the Lord's blessing on us. Begin by looking back on specific ways God has blessed over previous weeks. Though we may not fully realize what God has sown in our lives until a future harvest, the powerful nature of His Word can make a few accomplishments rapidly recognizable. As we spend the first half of our lesson glancing over our shoulders in a brief review, I pray that some will become apparent.

In the introductory session to our journey of ascent, we established that in God's economy the way up is down. Those of us who were willing made a commitment to daily (or regularly) take our places on our faces before God.

> **TODAY'S TREASURE**
> "May the LORD, Maker of heaven and earth, bless you from Zion."
> *Psalm 134:3, HCSB*

Reflect on your own experience of going face down. Did it have any impact on you? ○ yes ○ no *If so, describe how it affected you.*

PERSONAL QUESTION

In the introductory session and first lesson, we established three primary goals for this six-week Bible study. Review each one and reflect on ways those goals have been—or are in the process of being—accomplished.

God wants to raise us to a higher plain of worship and service. In our previous lesson we talked about the paramount outcome of an elevated worship life. A psalmist not only gives God praise but also pours out her heart in intimate disclosure.

1. How have you grown as a worshiper and psalmist in the last six weeks?

God desires to dramatically change our outlook on daily life. As we've echoed Psalm 84:5, God has been teaching us to set our hearts on pilgrimage (NIV).

2. *Which of the following is most accurate as our journey draws to conclusion?*
   ○ *I don't see life any differently than I did.*
   ○ *I think more often than I did about this life as pilgrimage and not destination.*
   ○ *I think often about pilgrimage and that this life—with all its hurts, losses, and challenges—is temporary. The new perspective is a significant help.*
   ○ *(Your own words if you prefer)* _____

God wants to usher us to the next step in our personal journeys with Him. Early on in our journey we celebrated the fact that those of us in Christ are never stuck. The revelation still excites me! When we began our journey, some of us may have felt exiled, captive to the enemy, and far from God, but now we're sensing some freedom. Though we've got a long way to go, some of us feel like we're back on the right road. Others of us may have entered the journey bored or busy and in need of a spiritual kick start and a personal revival. Still others may have realized that God wants them to take the next step in their serving life. Stepping up sometimes means stepping out. God is telling others that the time has come for them to finally take that step of faith they've wrestled over and prayed about long enough.

3. *What about you? In our climb up 15 stairs of ascent, have you recognized any specific area in which God was beckoning you to take the next step?*
   ○ *yes* ○ *no If so, please share it.*

_____

_____

One last review question before we take a fresh and concluding look at Psalm 134:3. Look at your stair graphic and note each description you wrote on Psalms 120–133. Hopefully, only the final one is blank. As you read each one, ask God to help you recollect the Psalm of Ascent it represents. Look back in your Bible if you'd like to stir your memory.

PRINCIPAL QUESTION

Now list three of the fifteen psalms that God used to speak most clearly to you and write the same statement beside each that you wrote on the stair graphic:

Psalm _____

Psalm _____

Psalm _____

I have reaped so much from our Psalms of Ascent, so much I wasn't even expecting! Indeed, as Psalm 134:3 says, the Lord, the Maker of heaven and earth, has blessed us from Zion. Kidner writes, "The word *bless* is perhaps the key-note of the psalm, sounded as it is in each verse. So far, it has been directed Godward; now it returns from God to man. But the exchange is quite unequal: to bless God is to acknowledge gratefully what He is; but to bless men, God must make of him what he is not, and give him what he has not."[21]

I could weep over the truth of those words. Yes, I have been greatly blessed. God has made me what I most certainly am not and given me what I have not.

What about you? What has God made you that you know you couldn't have been?

_____

What has He given you (beyond salvation) that you never would have possessed?

_____

The more we learn about God, the more we understand that the primary reason He asks us to surrender everything to Him is to make room to receive what He wants to give. Try as we may, we will never bring anything to God and leave empty handed unless we forget to take His gifts home. God's nature is to give.

Over and over in our study we've talked about becoming truer worshipers, actively blessing God. We cannot, however, bless God without being blessed disproportionately in return. As *Word Biblical Commentary* states, "Commitment is a two-way relationship, and so is blessing."[22] Since God's capacity infinitely exceeds ours, the same commentary calls the two-way blessing "a lopsided duality."[23]

In our previous lesson we talked about "doing what we came to do." Several of us felt convicted that sometimes we gather for worship and end up worshiping God in snippets and stolen moments between distractions. How blessed would we be today to realize that, as God calls us to "do what we came to do," His mind is also set on doing what He came to do? I believe God wants to increase our awareness that every time we bless Him He offers a disproportionate blessing to us. God doesn't consider us selfish and immature when we admit we want His blessing! He considers us obedient. If God wants to give a blessing, Dear One, I want to receive it. You too? Then let's look deeper into our text.

Read the three verses of Psalm 134 again so that you can recapture the context.

God's blessing can come in all sorts of ways but, based on the reference in Psalm 134:3 to the Lord as the Maker of heaven and earth, *Word Biblical Commentary* gives added emphasis to one blessing in particular. Picturing Psalm 134 as the benediction of blessing for gathered pilgrims in Jerusalem, it reads, "The worshipers will leave enriched and strengthened, with the invocation of divine blessing upon them ringing in their ears:

I have been greatly blessed. God has made me what I most certainly am not and given me what I have not.

'May that power which has been acknowledged in praise come flooding into your own lives!' "[24] They needed the reminder that the same God and the same great power that had been among them en masse would depart with each of them like a river splitting into ten thousand streams. Don't you and I need to know that right now? As we embrace and say good-bye after sharing a six-week pilgrimage to a feast of God's Word, don't we need to know that the same God we've sought and enjoyed together will remain with each of us as we part? I know I do.

What is your primary fear when a shared journey like this comes to an end?

We need to know that the same God we've sought and enjoyed together will remain with each of us as we part.

_____

Be well encouraged as *Word Biblical Commentary* proceeds to explain,

> "Zion is Yahweh's powerhouse: through it is channeled his own almighty power. Thus the extended description of the worshiping community in terms of space and time can now be replaced by a description of Yahweh as one who by right of creation controls both heaven and earth. Worship at Zion is a doorway that opens out into the power behind the world. Blessing extends in a remarkable cycle. Dynamic potential is given to those who sincerely acknowledge God's power. Essentially it is unsought and comes as a gracious byproduct of worship. In keeping with this attribute of power, the divine object of blessing becomes an active subject. God generously shares resources of omnipotence with devoted followers so that abundant life may be theirs."[25]

Wow! Underline God's part and circle the believer's part in that quote. Where could you use a blessing from the storehouse of God's omnipotence right now?

_____

I accidentally left my Bible at church one Sunday. It was my birthday and my Sunday School class members lavished me with so many gifts that my Bible didn't make it to the car. I felt almost physically ill until the church opened the next day and I could retrieve it. Oh, how many times have I've entered worship (at church, at home, in my car, at work) and blessed God with everything I had but then left the blessing God wanted to give me? Let's allow the words we just read to leap to life in us. Let's become keenly aware that we depart times of blessing God with blessings *from* God.

In just a few minutes we will conclude in what I hope will be a meaningful way. I pray that our perspectives have changed regarding the power of blessings we speak to God and over one another. After filling in your final line on the stair graphic, instead of writing your own rendition of Psalm 134, please think carefully about a blessing you'd like to speak over others. If you are in a small group, you'll be asked if you'd like to read your blessing over them as a benediction to your last gathering. If you are not in a small group, think of someone you'd like to speak a blessing over and write it for her or him. Here are the parameters: You must mean it and ask God sincerely to bestow it on them. At the end of this lesson write your blessing, limiting it to the space allowed. Brief blessings will be a necessity in small groups because each person will be invited to share. Even if you don't have a small group and you're just sharing it with one person, she or he will tend to remember and grasp it better if it is brief.

Thank you for taking this pilgrimage with me, Dear One. I have loved every single minute, and I was not ready for it to end. I'd like to pray a blessing over you that includes an image Keith painted in my mind in a voice mail yesterday. The parched land he leases in South Texas had received a rare downpour, and with great delight he watched a precious, wobbly-legged fawn with big brown eyes and oversized ears get mud on its hooves for the very first time. He said it jumped in the air, twirled around, and bucked like a miniature bronco until it shook every last bit of mud off its feet. I was completely grown before I realized that the mud I got on my feet from ditch-dwelling didn't belong there. I want something more for you.

My beloved sister in Christ … May God keep your heart set on pilgrimage. May He keep your eyes upon the destination and never let you forget that your Goal is a person, Jesus Christ, and He is waiting for you—in person—at your finish line. May you always remember what a great cloud of witnesses cheers you on in your journey to Mount Zion and bids you to "Be brave!" The race is not long, Beloved, so run hard! May your eyes be open to snares your enemy sets in your path and, should you tumble in the ditch, may your troubled heart be disallowed to condemn you. Jump in the air, twirl around, and buck like a bronco with repentance before your God until not a single speck of mud is left on your feet. Let God wash them in the water of His Word and plant them back on your path. When we feel heavy-laden in our journeys, may we check first to see if it's the burden of a swollen ego or the load of taking on a role that only belongs to God. May we lay down what has no place in our packs and run with the wind. When life is excruciating, may you find the strength in Christ to crawl on your hands and knees, sowing the Word of God and watering it with your tears. May you never forget that you are inconceivably loved and that God will prove infinitely faithful. And, on your way to the great feast in the heavenly Jerusalem, may you glance often to your right and to your left and offer a fellow pilgrim a helping hand. May the Lord, Maker of heaven and earth, bless you from Zion.

With deep affection—
Beth

May God keep your heart set on pilgrimage.

Your Blessing Upon Others: _____

_____

_____

viewer guide

SESSION SIX

Blessings from Zion

Today we conclude our journey together through the Psalms of Ascent. Our concluding thoughts will center on four ways to have the most satisfying pilgrimage possible.

Lamentations 1:4, The Message

1. See Jeremiah 31:21. _____ the _____ you are on.

   Philippians 1:9-10; Psalm 19:11

2. See Hebrews 12:1-2. _____ _____ of the _____

   God wants to _____.

3. See Psalm 84:1-7. Take the _____ _____ with the next strength.

   Compare Isaiah 40:28-31.

4. Conclude with Isaiah 35:3-10. Know with certainty that the

   _____ is _____ _____ _____.

   Psalm 134:3

Video sessions are available for download at www.lifeway.com/women.

173

Endnotes

WEEK ONE

1. Trent Butler, Chad Brand, Charles Draper, Archie England. *Holman Illustrated Bible Dictionary* (Nashville, TN: B&H Publishing Group, 2003), 1342.
2. Ibid.
3. Ibid.
4. John Calvin. *Commentary on The Book of Psalms* (Grand Rapids, MI: Baker Book House, 1998), xxxvii.
5. Loren D. Crowe. *The Songs of Ascents: Their Place in Israelite History and Religion* (Atlanta, GA: SBLDS, 1996), 33.
6. Hans-Joachim Kraus. *Psalms 60–150: A Continental Commentary* (Minneapolis: Augsburg Fortress Publishers, 1993), 446.
7. David G. Barker. *The LORD Watches Over You: A Pilgrimage Reading of Psalm 121,* Bibliotheca Sacra 152 (April–June 1995) Copyright © 1995 by Dallas Theological Seminary, 163-181.
8. David G. Barker article in reference to Ceresko's findings recorded in "Psalm 121: Prayer of a Warrior," 499.
9. Hayim Baltsan. *Webster's New World Hebrew Dictionary* (NY: Simon & Schuster, Inc., 1992), 385.
10. Mitchell Dagood. *Psalms 101–150 in The Anchor Bible,* (Garden City: NY: Doubleday and Company, Inc., 1970), 202.
11. Ibid.
12. Crowe, 45-46.
13. Leslie C. Allen. *Psalms 101–150 in Word Biblical Commentary,* Vol. 21 (Waco: Word Books Publisher, 1983), 158.

WEEK TWO

1. Leslie C. Mitchell. *Psalms 101–150 in Word Biblical Commentary,* Vol. 21 (Waco: Word Books Publisher, 1983), 157.
2. Eugene H. Peterson. *A Long Obedience in the Same Direction* (Downer's Grove, IL: InterVarsity Press, 2000), 63.
3. Samuel Terrien. *The Psalms: Strophic Structure and Theological Commentary* (Eerdman's Critical Commentary) (Grand Rapids, MI: William B. Eerdmans Publishing Company, 2003), 818.
4. John Eaton. *The Psalms: A Historical and Spiritual Commentary with an Introduction and a New Translation* (Continuum International Publishing Group, 2006), 428.
5. James Strong. *Strong's Exhaustive Concordance of the Bible.* (Nashville: Broadman & Holman Publishing, 1999), #937, 936.
6. Spiros Zodhiates, ed. *Hebrew-Greek Key Word Study Bible* (Chattanooga, TN: AMG Publishers, 1996), 1516.
7. Terrien, 818-819.
8. Peterson, 71.
9. Ibid.
10. Loren D. Crowe. *The Songs of Ascents: Their Place in Israelite History and Religion* (Atlanta, GA: SBLDS, 1996), 52-53.
11. Ibid., 53.
12. Ibid., 52.

WEEK THREE

1. Spiros Zodhiates, ed. *Hebrew-Greek Key Word Study Bible* (Chattanooga, TN: AMG, 1996), 1913.
2. James Limburg. "Psalms" in the *Westminster Bible Companion* (Louisville, KY: Westminster John Knox Press, 2000). 435.
3. Ibid.
4. Eugene Peterson. *A Long Obedience in the Same Direction* (Downer's Grove, IL: InterVarsity Press, 2000), 101.
5. James M. Boice. *Psalms, vol. 3* (Grand Rapids, MI: Baker Books, 1998), 1117.
6. Ibid., 1118.
7. Ibid., 1118.
8. Peterson, 109.
9. CNN. "Lack of sleep America's top health problem, doctors say" [online] March 17, 1997 [cited 23 April 2007]. Available on the Internet: *http://www.cnn.com/HEALTH/9703/17/nfm/sleep.deprivation/index.html.*
10. CNN. "Sleep deprivation as bad as alcohol impairment" [online] September 20, 2000 [cited 10 May 2007]. Available on the Internet: *http://archives.cnn.com/2000/HEALTH/09/20/sleep.deprivation.*
11. CNN. "Lack of sleep America's top health problem, doctors say" [online] March 17, 1997 [cited 23 April 2007]. Available on the Internet: *http://www.cnn.com/HEALTH/9703/17/nfm/sleep.deprivation/index.html.*

WEEK FOUR

1. James M. Boice. *Psalms, vol. 3* (Grand Rapids, MI: Baker Books, 1998), 1124.
2. Spiro Zodhiates, ed. *Hebrew-Greek Key Word Study Bible* (Chattanooga, TN: AMG Publishers, 1996),164.
3. Eugene H. Peterson. *A Long Obedience in the Same Direction* (Downer's Grove, IL: InterVarsity Press, 2000), 118.
4. Ibid.
5. James Strong. *The Strongest Strong's Exhaustive Concordance of the Bible* (Grand Rapids, MI: Zondervan, 2001), 1448.
6. Loren D. Crowe. *The Songs of Ascents: Their Place in Israelite History and Religion* (Atlanta, GA: SBLDS, 1996), 83.
7. Leslie C. Allen. *Psalms 101–150 in Word Biblical Commentary, vol. 21* (Waco: Word Books Publisher, 1983), 4.
8. Boice, 1130.
9. Derek Kidner. *Psalms 73-150* (London: InterVarsity Press, 1975), 444.
10. Boice, 1131.
11. Walter C. Kaiser. *Hard Sayings of the Bible* (Downer's Grove, IL: InterVarsity Press, 1996), 280.
12. Nahum Sarna. *On the Book of Psalms: Exploring the Prayers of Ancient Israel* (New York: Schocken, 1993), 3.
13. Kaiser, 281.

WEEK FIVE

1. Herbert Lockyer. *All the Divine Names and Titles in the Bible* (Grand Rapids, MI: Zondervan, 1975), 17.
2. Trent Butler, ed. *Holman Illustrated Bible Dictionary* (Nashville: Holman Bible Publishers, 1991), 684.
3. Leslie C. Allen. *Psalms 101–150 in Word Biblical Commentary, vol. 21* (Waco: Word Books Publisher, 1983), 197.
4. Spiro Zodhiates, ed. *Hebrew-Greek Key Word Study Bible* (Chattanooga, TN: AMG Publishers, 1996), 1548.
5. Ibid., 1619.
6. Allen, 198.
7. Boice, 1147.
8. Boice, 1149.
9. Allen, 198.
10. Allen, 197.
11. Allen, 197.
12. James Limburg. *Westminster Bible Companion* (Louisville, KY: Westminster John Knox Press, 2000) 452.
13. Ibid., 453.
14. Butler, 849.
15. Derek Kidner. *Psalms 73-150* (London: InterVarsity Press, 1975), 449.

WEEK SIX

1. James Limburg. "Psalms" in the *Westminster Bible Companion* (Louisville, KY: Westminster John Knox Press, 2000), 454.
2. James M. Boice. *Psalms, vol. 3.* (Grand Rapids: Baker Book House Co., 1998), 1156.
3. Geoffrey W. Bromiley, ed. *International Standard Bible Encyclopedia* (Grand Rapids, MI: William B. Eerdmans, 1979), 120.
4. Derek Kidner. *Psalms 73-150* (London: InterVarsity Press, 1975), 451.
5. Ibid., 451-52.
6. Leander Keck, ed. *New Interpreter's Bible, vol. 4* (Nashville: Abingdon Press, 1996), 1215.
7. Loren Crowe. *The Songs of Ascents: Their Place in Israelite History and Religion* (Atlanta, GA: SBLDS, 1996), 114.
8. Ibid.
9. Keck, 1214.
10. Eugene H. Peterson. *A Long Obedience in the Same Direction* (Downer's Grove, IL: InterVarsity Press, 2000), 178.
11. John Eaton. *The Psalms: A Historical and Spiritual Commentary with an Introduction and a New Translation* (Continuum International Publishing Group, 2006), 446.
12. Peterson, 184.
13. Dietrich Bonhoeffer. *Life Together* (New York: Harper & Row Publishers, Inc., 1954), 25.
14. Boice, 1166.
15. Keck, 1216.
16. Peterson, 193.
17. Charles A. Briggs, Emilie G. Briggs, ed. *The International Critical Commentary* (Edinburgh: T & T Clark, 1976), 476.
18. Leslie C. Allen. *Psalms 101–150 in Word Biblical Commentary, vol. 21* (Waco: Word Books Publisher, 1983), 218.
19. Karl Barth. *Church Dogmatics* (Edinburgh: T & T Clark, 1961), 4.
20. Peterson, 198.
21. Kidner, 454.
22. Allen, 218.
23. Ibid.
24. Ibid.
25. Ibid., 219.

Art & Photo Credits

Images photographed on location in Israel during the filming of Stepping Up. Cover photo by Micah Kandros. Temple model by *TempleModels.com*. Steps diagram by Dan Brawner. Interior design by Susan Browne and Jon Rodda. Collage art by Leigh Ann Dans and photographed by Randy Hughes. Interior photos by Micah Kandros: pages 4, 12, 22, 38, 42, 52, 56, 70, 75, 84, 97, 101, 111, 120, 130, 135, 139, 148, 153, 157, 162, 167. Interior photos by Jon Rodda: pages 17, 26, 30, 47, 66, 79, 92, 106, 125. All images © 2007, LifeWay Christian Resources.

CHRISTIAN GROWTH STUDY PLAN

In the Christian Growth Study Plan *Stepping Up: A Journey through the Psalms of Ascent* is a resource for course credit in the subject area Personal Life in the Christian Growth category of plans. To receive credit, read the book; complete the learning activities; attend group sessions; show your work to your pastor, a staff member, or a church leader; then complete this form. This page may be duplicated. Send the completed form to:

Christian Growth Study Plan; One LifeWay Plaza, Nashville, TN 37234-0117; Fax (615) 251-5067; e-mail *cgspnet@lifeway.com*. For information about the Christian Growth Study Plan, refer to the current *Christian Growth Study Plan Catalog,* located online at *www.lifeway.com/cgsp*. If you do not have access to the Internet, contact the Christian Growth Study Plan office, (800) 968-5519, for the specific plan you need for your ministry.

STEPPING UP
COURSE NUMBER: CG-1303

PARTICIPANT INFORMATION

Social Security Number (USA ONLY-optional)   –   –

Personal CGSP Number*   –

Date of Birth (MONTH, DAY, YEAR)   –   –

Name (First, Middle, Last)

Home Phone   –   –

Address (Street, Route, or P.O. Box)

City, State, or Province

Zip/Postal Code

Email Address for CGSP use

Please check appropriate box: ❑ Resource purchased by church   ❑ Resource purchased by self   ❑ Other

CHURCH INFORMATION

Church Name

Address (Street, Route, or P.O. Box)

City, State, or Province

Zip/Postal Code

CHANGE REQUEST ONLY

❑ Former Name

❑ Former Address   City, State, or Province   Zip/Postal Code

❑ Former Church   City, State, or Province   Zip/Postal Code

Signature of Pastor, Conference Leader, or Other Church Leader   Date

*New participants are requested but not required to give SS# and date of birth. Existing participants, please give CGSP# when using SS# for the first time. Thereafter, only one ID# is required. **Mail to:** Christian Growth Study Plan, One LifeWay Plaza, Nashville, TN 37234-0117. Fax: (615)251-5067.

Revised 4-05